André Gide *circa* 1914

ANDRÉ GIDE:
THE EVOLUTION OF AN AESTHETIC

by VINIO ROSSI

La réalité m'a donné la direction
et l'élan; mon imagination fait le reste. Elle
n'invente rien, mais travaille sans cesse dans le
prolongement des *données*.

Journal,
July 11, 1926

RUTGERS UNIVERSITY PRESS
New Brunswick   *New Jersey*

*Manufactured in the United States of America
by Quinn & Boden Company, Inc., Rahway, N.J.*

Permission for the use of the publications listed below has
been kindly granted by the following publishers:

Editions Gallimard—André Gide: *Les Cahiers d'André
Walter, Le Traité du Narcisse, Le Voyage d'Urien, La
Tentative amoureuse,* in *Oeuvres Complètes d'André Gide*
(1932–1939), © Gallimard; André Gide: *Journal, 1889–
1949, Souvenirs* © Gallimard; André Gide: "Préface pour
la deuxième édition du *Voyage d'Urien*" and "Postface
pour la deuxième édition de *Paludes,*" in *Romans, récits, et
soties, oeuvres lyriques* (1959), © Gallimard; and Jean
Delay: *La Jeunesse d'André Gide* (1956–1957), © Gallimard.

Alfred A. Knopf, Inc.—*Journal, 1889–1949,* tr. Justin
O'Brien.

New Directions Publishing Corporation—André Gide:
Paludes (from *Oeuvres Complètes d'André Gide*). Printed
by permission of New Directions Publishing Corporation,
publishers of *Marshlands and Prometheus Misbound,* copy-
right 1953 by New Directions.

Martin Secker and Warburg, Ltd. (English translator)—
André Gide: *Paludes* (from *Oeuvres Complètes d'André
Gide*); *Journal, 1889–1949.*

University of Chicago Press (original English translator)—
Jean Delay: *La Jeunesse d'André Gide* (1956–1957).

Acknowledgement is made to Henri Jonquières, publisher, for
the frontispiece, which is a reproduction of a sketch appearing
in André Gide: *Dostoievski* (1928).

for Anne

Preface

In 1889, at the age of twenty, André Gide set out to write his "oeuvres complètes." He began thinking in terms of his complete works, cultivating his life in view of a future biography, transforming everything into a long, varied, and continuous statement about himself and his reactions to the world about him. In May of that year, he remarked that "my whole life's work is grouping itself, is falling into place with such unity that I cannot doubt that I will see it accomplished." Even then Gide did not consider any single one of his future works (including *Les Cahiers d'André Walter*, the "*summa*" of his youth) as an end in itself, dissociated from the whole. Rather, he imagined each work as an aesthetically independent unit that would interact with others in the context of the future "oeuvres complètes," where the progression and succession, the implicit readjustment of form and content from one work to the next would be more meaningful and significant than the beauty and perfection of any one alone. Four years later, in a letter to Marcel Drouin, Gide declared that he saw his complete works as a shelf of books, each one appearing, as the years went by, not one after another, but in the spaces reserved for those to come, now before, now after those already in print.

In 1926, when he was almost sixty and still had twenty-five years more to live and write, Gide felt ready to join those who have seen the accomplishment of what they had set out to do. "When I examine my life, the dominant characteristic

I find is not inconstancy at all but, on the contrary, fidelity."
This does not mean that, forty years earlier, Gide had in mind
the form and substance of such varied works as *Paludes, La
Porte étroite, Souvenirs de la Cour d'Assises, Les Faux-
Monnayeurs,* and *Corydon.* "No one can know," he continued
in his 1893 letter, "what I have to say except myself, and to
know it, even I need all my meditations." Nor does fidelity
imply that his life had been based on an a priori notion of
what he was and what he was to achieve. It simply suggests
that he had more or less intuited his literary domain and, more
significantly, that he had envisaged his entire work as a unified
corpus whose separate parts would no more faithfully represent him than would any act or remark, in the course of a
lifetime, taken alone and out of context. His fidelity was to
his own being, to a program of constant exploration and
expression of all the facets of his personality, to the deliberate
and always renewed effort to shape his life and work.

But, in 1893, Gide was not yet ready to undertake a major
project. "I think I see what you expect from me," he tells
Drouin, "and I'm sure I'll write it. But those are projects for
my thirties. I still have six more years of prefaces." These
"prefaces" to the "oeuvres complètes," from *Les Cahiers
d'André Walter* (1891) to *Paludes* (1895) and the pamphlet,
Réflexions sur quelques points de littérature et de morale
(1897), are the major concern of the pages that follow. But
instead of considering his search for *what* to say, they are
primarily concerned with his attempt to find *how* to say it.
The refinement of a style, of a form, Gide was to realize later
in life, frequently solves both problems. But the process can
be tedious. Although these "prefaces" are far from being the
most fascinating of Gide's works, they are nevertheless quite
readable and interesting as testimonies of a particular period
and a particular personality. More important, they are docu-
ments which record the progress Gide made as a young artist

struggling to master his craft. It is frequently the early or least successful works that help us to understand the aspirations of a great artist, the way he reconciles them with his talent, the functioning of his imagination, and the development of his art.

In general, of course, prefaces introduce, defend, or prepare the way for what is to follow. It is the purpose of this study to analyze *Les Cahiers d'André Walter, Le Traité du Narcisse, Le Voyage d'Urien, La Tentative amoureuse, Paludes,* and finally, *Réflexions sur quelques points de littérature et de morale* in order to trace Gide's imaginative processes and fictional techniques in their evolution towards the formal perfection attained first in *Paludes* and evident in all his mature work. Thus, in my last chapter, the major works such as *L'Immoraliste, La Porte étroite, La Symphonie pastorale,* and *Les Faux-Monnayeurs* are considered from the vantage point of the earlier exposition. For the principles of composition evolved between 1890–97 can be considered as *bona fide* guides only insofar as they support and sustain analysis of the later masterpieces. This study rests, then, on the assumption that Gide's early work is the basis for his *Oeuvres complètes*; that "the reader will be able to judge one part with justice only after having become acquainted with the whole—that is, after I'm gone—for every act of our lives is in a way a preface or an announcement of those to follow." (Letter to Marcel Drouin, 1893.)

Wherever feasible, I have substituted in the text of the essay translations of French material. I include in the notes translations of those quotations I deemed necessary to reproduce in the original. With few exceptions, specifically where a translator is indicated in the notes, the translations are my own. They are by no means polished and are intended only as working versions.

For their careful reading and numerous suggestions, I thank

Preface

Professors Leroy C. Breunig, Gilbert Highet, Jean Hytier, and Leon S. Roudiez. Professor Justin O'Brien read and re-read the manuscript from sketch to working version; with him and because of him, the study gained shape and substance. I thank, too, my colleague, Professor John K. Hyde, for his valuable comments. But the final form is, of course, my own responsibility. My warm thanks to M. Jacques Naville and to the Comité Gide for permission to consult and quote unpublished material in the Fonds Gide of the Bibliothèque littéraire Jacques Doucet in Paris. Anne Rossi compiled the index, but her hand also appears in all that precedes it.

V.R.

Florence, 1966

Contents

Preface   v

Introduction   3

I   *Les Cahiers d'André Walter:* Ambitions and
    Realizations   17

II   The Symbol: Practice and Theory   38

III   *Le Voyage d'Urien:* Gide's Pathetic Fallacy   63

IV   Two Images: The Egg of the Cuttlefish and the
    Swamp   82

V   The Critical Works   99

VI   The Keyhole Metaphor and the Parable   124

VII   Conclusion: The A Priori Novel   144

Notes   163

A Selected Bibliography   187

Index   195

ANDRÉ GIDE:

THE EVOLUTION OF AN AESTHETIC

Introduction

Surreptitiously observing the festivities at a gala party, the four-year-old André Gide felt himself being initiated into a new life, quite different, quite mysterious, and more stimulating than life until then. "The indistinct, indefinable belief in something else existing alongside the real, daily, acknowledged world," he recalls in *Si le Grain ne meurt*, "dwelled in me for a number of years." [1] This belief grew in intensity through his adolescence and early manhood. His first trip to North Africa in the fall of 1893, his twenty-fourth year, was a turning point in his life; his sudden illness and subsequent reawakening to sensual experience seemed to reverse his previous psychological attitude towards reality. He now attempted to negate his past and to affirm a distinct belief in the reality of immediate phenomena. But, while the experience was important, the reversal was neither permanent nor profound. Despite the months in Biskra, despite his eulogy of the fruits of the earth, he did not fully succeed in changing himself. He could not become a hedonist.

Gide's youthful willingness to posit another reality arose from persistent difficulties with this world. In his journals, memoirs, and other nonfiction, he frequently remarked that he was unable to cope with it or even believe entirely in its existence. A false move, he felt, would send him through the set and backstage, [2] or crashing through a fragile glass floor. [3] This feeling remained with him to the very end of his life. In *Ainsi soit-il ou Les Jeux sont faits*, Gide refers to it

3

again, perhaps for the last time. In answer to Valéry's statement that events do not interest him, Gide says that he is interested, indeed even expects to take part in what happens. "But, to tell the truth, I have to admit that I do not really manage to believe in it . . . I do not adhere, I have never been able to *adhere* perfectly to reality." [4]

As he implies, his inability to believe completely in the exterior world never prevented him from acting, from being involved in what was about him; indeed at times it enabled him to act quickly and even valiantly in emergencies. His dissociation allowed him to remain calm and in control of dangerous or difficult situations.[5] But if this distance was helpful in keeping him from being touched by the urgency of the present, it had its disadvantages when he wanted contact with a more general, everyday reality.

In his excellent psychobiography, *La Jeunesse d'André Gide,* Jean Delay briefly mentions the partial dissociation from reality as symptomatic of a mental disorder Gide suffered from. But he does not explore very far into Gide's problematic relationship with the real world, a grasp of which is essential to an understanding of Gide's art and to full appreciation of both its strength and weakness.

Because an artist normally involves his entire being in fulfilling his self-imposed function, and because Gide not only involved himself completely but also drew heavily upon the facts and events of his life for his art, many critics of his entire work have justly fused biography and literary criticism. The two cannot be separated in any extended study of his work: Gide lived his novels as though they were life. Too timid or too weak psychologically to become involved in the strain of reality, he withdrew into his imagination, into a safe inner world, where he carried on with less effort and energy the necessary testing, reacting, and modifying of behavior. But he was not a hermit; he spent a great deal of time with friends, in Paris and on frequent trips. Throughout his life he circulated in society with apparent ease. Still, his activities at the moment of their occurrence touched him only intellectually. It was afterwards, in his imagination and then in his writings, that he proved able to experience these activities more completely and to experiment with the alternatives of human behavior.

The French psychologist, Pierre Janet, gives some hints as to the mechanics of this withdrawal. In a series of lectures entitled *L'Evolution de la mémoire et de la notion du temps,*[6] he firmly ties this lack of the feeling of reality to a deformed sense of time and, ultimately, to an inability to experience the present. Briefly, to paraphrase Janet, the sense of the present requires a running narrative to oneself of an action's inception, duration, and completion, simultaneously with the completion of the action itself. This narrative fixes in the subject's mind the action he has begun, endured, and completed; it is the means by which he experiences and possesses his completed act.[7] (One might cite as examples the running commentaries made by children upon the activities they are engrossed in, or even by adults when distracted or involved in an absorbing task; in these cases the usually subconscious narrative momentarily rises to the conscious level.) Only through this narrative is duration experienced, along with its implied beginnings and endings (since without the beginnings and endings the notion of duration is nonsense, just as the notion of life cannot be comprehended without the attendant ideas of birth and death). So a precise sense of time's passage depends not only upon the action begun, endured, and completed but also upon the attendant cognitive narrative which defines and fixes the present in the subject's mind. Janet calls this cycle "la présentification."[8]

For those unable to recognize and thus possess this cycle,

time is deformed; they experience it in a different manner. Such people may nevertheless record experience, but never directly. Immediate experience apparently becomes transferred to the past almost upon occurrence and is apprehended by something analogous to memory. Time, therefore, is a vague notion; past and future may be somehow sensed but without any clear differentiation between actions just passed and long passed, or between the imminent and the far-off future. Consequently, the general sense of time, and ultimately of reality, is greatly undermined. The sense of direct contact with things and events is lost and experience is removed to a cerebral realm. Thus, in effect, the psychasthenic places a screen between himself and the world.[9]

In the remainder of the very important passage of *Ainsi soit-il* concerning Valéry's remark, Gide echoes some of Janet's observations. Guessing at the possible reason for his uncertain belief in reality, he states: "I believe this deficiency (for, obviously, it is one) must be linked with what I was saying earlier, the deficiency in my sense of time. I immediately put into the past whatever happens to me or to others."[10] We can imagine Gide withdrawing to his study to meditate, to digest the day's events, turning them over in his imagination. For it was in his imagination that Gide was able to experience contact with a reality analogous to the one from which he felt apart.

> Everything happens as if the necessary effort to affirm, to decide, to act, required an abnormal expenditure of energy from his nervous system. But this changes as soon as he substitutes the world of imagination and representation for that of reality and action. The immediate adaptation to the present, to reality, to society exhausts his weak nervous system, but his resources seem to be unlimited when he turns to interior analysis.[11]

Introduction

We take Jean Delay's expression "interior analysis" to mean both analysis *in* the interior as well as analysis *of* the interior of Gide's personality. Delay selects only the latter meaning, and delves into the narcissistic aspects of Gide's withdrawal to the interior of his consciousness. But he withdrew not only in order to realize an ideal self but also to experience contact with himself and with life. Analysis or contemplation of himself *in vivo*, within the confines of a selective consciousness, afforded him a means to experience this contact, though at second hand. Although in both cases the return to the self was motivated by different and opposing reasons, the return itself was an evasion of reality, in the final analysis. Such an evasion can prove highly dangerous to one's mental stability. For if the world of the imagination is easier to deal with, the danger of permanent dissociation from the real world is all the stronger. What saved Gide was his art. For, as Freud knew and as Jean Delay states, art, as expression, leads back to reality because it is objectification.[12]

In this light the double impulse of Gide's withdrawal is important to the understanding of his art. For as his work became less the realm of self-idealization, it became more the realm of experience. Whether he served on a jury or travelled through the jungle, flirted with communism or with Catholicism, all was transcribed and assimilated, all was concretized through literature. In order to experience, to cope with a reality whose complexity was threatening, Gide had to reorganize it in his own terms.

I immediately put into the past whatever happens to me or to others. This is enough to falsify seriously the judgment of events destined to have historical significance. I bury people and things, and even myself, with disconcerting ease. From all this I retain (oh, quite despite myself)

7

only the meaning. And at the rate at which the world is going, I constantly tell myself and repeat that these ratiocinations might very well be swept away before long with all the rest. But I write them down nonetheless.[18]

To use Janet's terms, Gide put his running interior monologue into the past tense, so that present perceptions immediately became analogous to remembered ones. In this process he eliminated the continuity of experience, and distilled it instead into "ratiocinations" or little nodules of history. Thus, for him, the past was not a steady flow but a collection of independent units. The immediate conscious impact of an event consisted not of a total sensory awareness but, instead, of the intellectual significance with which he instantaneously imbued it. These nodules could be later reactivated and frequently were for the purposes of his *Journal.* Since his aesthetic sensibility inevitably entered into their reactivation, the process was tantamount to a re-creation of the original experiences and necessarily involved the creative act. Thus, moved more often by the exigencies of aesthetic or emotional validity than by objective fact, Gide's expressed recollection of events does not always coincide with the report from other sources of the same events. Consider, for example, one of his first recollections mentioned in *Si le Grain ne meurt,* the entrance of the Prussians into Rouen. Assured by his mother, upon examination of this memory, that he was too young to remember the event (he was barely more than a year old in December, 1870), and that he had confused it with a less spectacular parade staged by the Rouennais themselves, he nevertheless felt disappointed:

it seemed to me that I was closer to the truth at first and that the event which my completely new senses endowed with so much importance indeed deserved to be an historic event. From this arose my unconscious need to push it very far back in time in order that it be magnified by distance.[14]

This memory was relegated to a strange region of his consciousness where truth was more a matter of feeling than of fact. Relegated to this same region was the memory of the gala party at the home of his aunt and uncle in Rouen. The juxtaposition of these two episodes in *Si le Grain ne meurt* is not fortuitous; both deal with Gide's dissociation from reality. For it was his unsureness with the real world that led him to believe he was being initiated into a new life when he watched the proceedings of the "bal, rue de Crosne." It is true that the ball was not an everyday event. But Gide set it far above reality and endowed it with supra-real qualities.

There is reality and there are dreams; and then there is *a second reality*,[15]

he concludes in his memoirs, a reality closer to the truth, more emotionally unified and consistent than the real world he imperfectly perceived.

The ball appealed to him because of its artificiality, the deliberate attempt on the part of the participants to live life, however momentarily, on an idealized plane. But this second reality is by no means to be confused with the fantastic world of goblins, ghouls, and witches, or even with that of Hoffmann or Andersen. "No," Gide tells us in *Si le Grain ne meurt*,

I think, rather, that what was in question was an awkward need to make life more dense, a need that religion would satisfy later; and also, a certain inclination to imagine the clandestine.[16]

His need to make his life more dense stemmed from the inadequacy he felt in his existence. He understood that he did not "possess" reality as others do, that his experience of it was little more than a thin intellectual filtrate. But he could cope with it because it had none of the complexity and diversity that characterize life. His experience, he reasoned, was thus an abstract of life and contained its essence. The realm of consciousness in which he habitually lived and in which he formed his nodules of experience became eventually, in his mind, a part of a larger construct which exists beyond our senses and of which we can have only incomplete knowledge.[17] This construct was the supra-reality, the true and ideal world that lay hidden by the everyday world of appearances. Encouraged at first by his conviction that he was among the chosen, by his Christian upbringing and religious fervor, and later on by his adherence to the Symbolist doctrine, he gave full credence to the metaphysical value of his construct, even though it was essentially a construct of his imagination. The only outlet for Gide's imagination was the rational region of the consciousness, where he ordered and reduced all experience to apprehensible elements which he consequently imbued with symbolic significance. It was, for Gide, the aesthetic realm par excellence, the realm in which thought and logic create.

But Gide was by no means as coldly intellectual as might be suggested by this description. High-strung and nervous and extremely sensual, he early compounded in himself all the vague yet intense emotions and aspirations that characterize adolescents unable to find suitable outlets in the everyday world. His rigorously Protestant upbringing, combined with a physiological hypersensitivity, formed the basis of his difficulty. Brought up to be suspicious of all sensual intercourse with the world and constantly alert for any pitfall of this sort, he had erected, even before adolescence, a subconscious barrier to safeguard himself against the guilt that might arise from contact with his own sensations. To compensate for what was lacking, he intensified his life by abandoning himself to the religious fervor of his adolescence. But, as he noted later in *Les Cahiers d'André Walter*, this fervor, too, teetered on the brink of sensuality, and was therefore as dangerous as any physical contact. All of this, it should be noted, was on a subconscious level; during most of his adolescence, Gide was consciously aware only of the intensity of his emotions. He did not realize that he required an outlet that his intellect, his only active link to reality, could not offer. Therefore, he found himself at an impasse. Without a satisfying means of diffusion, his emotions welled up inside him to an explosive intensity, to be detonated only years later in North Africa.

Before he discovered the Symbolists in 1891, Gide's ideas of art were based, for the most part, on the approaches to literature prevalent in the nineteenth century, all of which presupposed a rigorous observation, scrutiny, and manipulation of the events of daily life. Balzac, Flaubert, Zola, among the most prominent figures, relied heavily upon their perceptions of the contemporary world for the raw material of their books. Flaubert, we remember, was impelled to observe at first hand the setting of *Salammbô* with the expectation of producing a work fraught with verisimilitude. The technique all these writers upheld with passion was the faithful representation of reality. But Gide's very special psychological makeup rendered ineffectual such an attempt to transform reality into art and eventually made it distasteful to him. Moreover, his prime preoccupation was his own imprecise and complex emotion seeking very precise expression. As a result, his first literary efforts were too personal and subjective to allow the reader any meaningful identification with the intense feelings depicted. It is true that the Realists and Naturalists ended by presenting a personal vision of contemporary reality in their works, despite all their efforts at objectivity.[18] But Gide, at first, was incapable of presenting any vision of the world since he had no experience to speak of save that of himself.

Although writing became Gide's road to stability, it was a long while before it satisfied his psychological and aesthetic needs to any great degree. Before art could offer such satisfaction Gide had to come to terms with both reality and his own emotions. After the failure of *Les Cahiers d'André Walter*, he realized the importance a visceral apprehension of reality would have for his art. For the unhampered perception of the real world provides the substance of an expressive vocabulary not normally afforded by the analytical and rational elements of language alone. The basic unit of such a vocabulary is the image. As a picture in words of an object in the real world, it has, among other qualities, "some trace of the sensuous in it." As such it necessarily presupposes on the part of the image-maker an intimate knowledge of that object. Since Gide lacked the capacity for this intimacy, the nature of his images necessarily reflects the limited nature of his relationship with the world. But the image is more than just a picture in words; it is "to some degree metaphorical, with an undernote of some human emotion in its content." [19] In his need to express his pent-up emotions, Gide allowed his feelings to drown his frail experience instead of sustaining it. His struggle was to keep from overloading his impressions of the world with his own emotions and, instead, to permit the world to act upon him. Thus, the development of his imagery reflects his attempts at reconciliation with phenomena.

To the end of his life, Gide continued to "inform" objects, both artistic and natural, instead of being informed by them. This, within limits, is as it should be if the original writer is to share with us his vision of the world. But the expression, "vision of the world," suggests a compromise between its two elements, one that Gide was able to effect in art with great effort, and only after several failures. At the beginning of his career, he presents little more than a vision of himself in a world very nearly transformed beyond recognition by his inadequacies and the compensations they provoked.

In this light, Gide's toying with the proverb, "man proposes and God disposes," in the 1901 essay, "Les Limites de l'art," assumes a more profoundly personal meaning than is apparent at first. Reversing the two propositions, he states that in the work of art, "God proposes and man disposes"; still, he is quick to insist that both be taken into account, for alone each proposition represents an artistic heresy: realism on the one hand, and idealism on the other. The latter was his most frequent temptation, even after he had learned that art is born only from the opposition of the two extremes. The novelist Edouard of *Les Faux-Monnayeurs* articulates in general terms the very conflict Gide had both to provoke and resolve with each of his creative attempts.

> I invent a novelist whom I set up as the central figure, and the subject of the book, if you will, is precisely the struggle between what reality offers him and what he means to make of it.[20]

One of the basic creative problems for most artists is precisely the struggle between reality and the idealization each seeks to make of it. But, for Gide, it was constant and conscious, crystallized by his psychological handicaps and at the same time infinitely complicated by them.

In order to resolve this problem, Gide had to find or invent a fictional form that most fully exploited those limited areas in which he could freely function. His inability to manipulate the objects and the events of the real world constantly frustrated his need to give vent to his emotions. This frustrated need, in turn, made contact with phenomena all the more urgent and, consequently, all the more difficult. Something had to yield. After much experimentation, the breakthrough occurred quite accidentally with an image in *La Tentative amoureuse*. Prompted by a change in mood, this opened the way for the full development of Gide's first major image: the swamp of *Paludes*. Both satisfy the definitions of the image offered by C. Day Lewis; but, more important, they represent a breakthrough because they are the earliest that are not overpowered by Gide's emotions. In the realm of aesthetics, and in particular with reference to the image, Gide first learned the lesson of the biblical aphorism he was to paraphrase so frequently in his works: "He who loves his life loses it, and he who hates his life in this world will keep it for eternal life" (John XII:25). He learned to control his emotions and to abstain from deliberately infusing them into all he wrote. And he learned, too, how to substitute, with a certain measure of effectiveness, his limited experience for the intimate contact with reality he sorely lacked.

But art requires more than an isolated image, however successful or striking it may be. It must function in a larger context, or be handled in a significant way. Gide was unable to produce fresh and meaningful images; but once images were obtained, by whatever means and however banal, he could make them work effectively so long as he held his emotions in check and remained within the limits of his imagination. In his personal aesthetic realm, he easily brought to bear upon the handling of a given image his intellect and critical sense. By stripping an image of any personal feeling, he elevated it to a universal level; by limiting himself to it, expanding it, and organizing its elements into a logical development, he found a way to stylize reality in literature.

In his treatment of the image, Gide's guideline became the concrete object that yielded it; but he could never lose sight of its metaphorical undertones. These undertones, usually the first in most works of art to be critically perceived, give meaning to the image and carry the burden of conveying the author's ideas. Image and idea are, of course, inseparable; by insisting upon the logical development of an image, Gide invites us to consider the cogency of the idea it incorporates. In so fusing image and idea, aesthetics and ethics, Gide created a personal form of fiction that is both challenging and poetic. This form, first achieved in *Paludes*, is the modern parable.

I

Les Cahiers d'André Walter:
Ambitions and Realizations

For many a writer, it is his imagination working upon his own experience that furnishes the substance of his art. Camus, Montherlant, and even Gide himself are among the many who have been obliged to deny the imputation that their works are essentially autobiographical; they have often stated that the artist works with the various possibilities or potentialities of his life and experiences but is rarely limited to what has happened. But his own experience remains nevertheless the raw material of his art, and because experience entails, to a large extent, intercourse with the world, reality enters inevitably into the activity of literary creation. The writer has the ability to work with experience, to perceive in a particular event not only its value but the multiplicity of its untried possibilities and implications. The immediate and total perception of such relationships may be described as "intuition."

Now intuition is other than, if not the opposite of, reason. It may be defined as a nonrational activity of the mind wherein the faculty of reasoning is suspended and replaced by a highly sensitive perceptual power of obtaining knowledge. Unlike reason, which is aggressive and which yields limited fragmentary knowledge, intuition results in concrete knowledge of the world as an interrelated whole. Of the mental faculties that enter into the inspiration of a work of art, intuition plays a most important role, for the immediate and unhampered contact with reality yields the substance of art. Gide's ambition to be a poet was greatly inhibited by his incapacity for such involvement. Since he was in the habit of putting nearly all his experience into intellectual terms, his early attempts to convey emotion achieved little of the evocative power he sought; they were cold, analytical, and cramped by metrical difficulties. Later in life, when he had already evolved his aesthetic and delineated his literary domain, he did attain a certain lyrical quality in his prose. In the early years, however, he was frequently and deeply vexed by the problem of transposing rational and conceptual experience into a lyrical form normally requiring perceptual, "visceral" experience. His inability to solve this problem satisfactorily is at the root of the self-conscious zealousness that characterizes his early works. Lacking the experience and vocabulary necessary to evoke the emotions he felt, Gide clutched with naive insistence at any detail having even the remotest kinship to his feelings. This was especially so in *Les Cahiers d'André Walter*. The significance of this clutching may be clarified partly by considering his notions of the work of art, and partly by closer scrutiny of *Les Cahiers* themselves, his first completed work.

Gide attributes his philosophical initiation to Schopenhauer, whom he read and reread, he says in his memoirs, with unfailing diligence. In the unpublished "Cahier de notes de lectures" (1889–1902), he lists Schopenhauer's *The World as Will and Idea* on several occasions, stating rather candidly that "ç'aura été je crois ma plus grande influence." [1] Although he read both volumes of the French version available, he mentions the first alone on three separate occasions: May and July, 1890, and September, 1891. This volume, and undoubtedly Book III, which it contains, moved him to comment upon its influence on his thinking. In this section of his book, Schopenhauer discusses in detail various art forms and genres and their relationship to reality. His point of departure, which ties aesthetics to his central thesis, is the distinction between rational and intuitive knowledge. The terms he chose to characterize each type are rendered into English by " concept" and "Idea." Whereas the concept is abstract and expository, *unitas post rem*, the Idea "is always the object of perception" (i.e., intuition), the *unitas ante rem*. Moreover, if the concept is the "unity reconstructed out of multiplicity by the abstraction of our reason," the Idea is more elusive. It is known "only by him who has raised himself above all willing and all individuality to the pure subject of knowing" (contemplation). The Idea, then, is attained only by the man of genius who, by renouncing individuality, renders himself capable of perceiving the Idea intuitively.[2] Now, the objective of all art is the expression of this Idea, and the process whereby it is made perceptible to all men is, of course, the central problem of art. The artist attempts to order his readers' thinking in such a way as to enable them to perceive the Idea and re-create for themselves the artist's intuitive experience. Because the poet's medium is language, a conceptual phenomenon, he must needs employ conceptual material in order to communicate his percept. He does this by skillfully manipulating all that language is capable of, conceptually, rhythmically, and sonorously.

As the chemist obtains solid precipitates by combining perfectly clear and transparent fluids, the poet understands how to precipitate, as it were, the concrete, the individual, the perceptible, out of the abstract and transparent universality of the concepts by the manner in which he combines them. For the Idea can only be known by perception; and knowledge of the Idea is the end of art.[3]

Let us set aside the questions of rime and rhythm, for although they play an integral part in the total evocation of the Idea they eluded Schopenhauer's grasp. He was unable to comprehend their true value in a work of art and saw them merely as attention-catchers and -sustainers. He did grasp, however, the importance of another asset of language: though a conceptual phenomenon, it nevertheless has untold force as an image-maker.[4] As any handbook of poetry will affirm, the image may be used for itself, as a simple picture in words, or as a means to evoke a mood, a thought, an emotion, an idea. To this end it can be used in conjunction with other images, or alone but invested with some special attendant feeling. It may be used as a simile, as a metaphor, or when the distance between the vehicle and the tenor of a metaphor is infinitesimal—that is, when the two merge—a symbol. Now part of the intuitive process is the discovery of vehicles for the expression of an idea; it entails the perception of new or special relationships, and the investing of common phenomena with new or special significance. For the communication of a percept, poets have isolated and exaggerated aspects of exterior phenomena which facilitate comprehension of their experience. Consider, for example, the description of landscapes in the works of such different authors as Rousseau, Flaubert, or Hemingway. This preoccupation with the image as a communicative device can be exaggerated to the point of denying all other value of the real world except that of providing potential correspondences with the internal world of the poet. In a statement which could have been made by Mallarmé himself, Gide claims to see no reason for discerning the objects of reality if no emotion "fecundates" them: "il faut peindre le paysage et le phenomène seulement dans son rapport avec l'âme." [5] But even for Mallarmé, who scorned the world of contingency, contemplation of these objects was necessary in order to perceive their relationships with the soul. The symbol- or image-making process of the poet, then, requires the same visceral contact with reality that is essential for intuition. It is an integral part of the poet's craft and presupposes the ability "to see into the nature of things," that is, the capacity for poetic intuition.

Sensing the need for this sort of direct intuitive contact with the world about him and being unable to effect this contact, Gide was at a loss to fulfill his hopes of becoming a poet and of realizing the cry of his adolescence: "It is a poet that I want to be! It is a poet that I am!" [6] The facility of his friend Pierre Louÿs soon made him aware of his own failing and he sought the reason for it.

> I was . . . tormented by a constant desire for poetry but nothing was more embarrassed than my muse. All my efforts strove "to translate into verse" thoughts which I endowed with too much importance. . . . I let myself be frightfully cramped by rimes; far from being accompanied, guided, sustained by them, my emotion spent itself in pursuing them; and up until then, I had not been able to turn out anything worthwhile. [7]

Although these lines from *Si le Grain ne meurt* were written many years later, Gide understood at the time the nature of the aesthetic problem that was to haunt him for the rest of his life: the transference of intellectual material into a form that normally requires intuitive knowledge. The formal exigencies of French poetry further complicated the problem. In the unpublished part of his early journal he frequently alludes to his difficulty with verse and at one point simply gives up the struggle; "avec le vers," he explains, "on est trop esclave." [8] Earlier, while Gide and Pierre Louÿs were still in school, they had decided to exchange verses; unable to back out, Gide conjured up a mediocre poem whose first stanza he read to his friend.

J'ai voulu lui parler, il ne m'a pas compris.
Quand j'ai dit que j'aimais, il s'est mis à sourire.
J'aurais dû mieux choisir les mots pour le lui dire,
De mon amour secret feindre quelque mépris,
Ne pas paraître ému, peut-être même en rire.[9]

"The rest was worth nothing," he tells us after having quoted this effort, "and I was furious to feel it so. But, as I told Pierre Louÿs in order to excuse my awkwardness, a book, a projected book, dwelled in my heart above all else . . . distracted me from anything else. It was *André Walter*." [10]

It is interesting to note the excuse for his slight poetic attempt: the imperious demands of his first book. He had been thinking of writing a novel for some time, and the subject, or theme, was already fixed in his mind. Throughout the year 1888–1889 he nourished his projected book with all his interrogations, doubts, troubles, with his love, above all, which was the pivot for everything else.

That he was actually writing the book, however, is at best doubtful, although he was keeping a journal at the time, some of whose entries later found their way into *Les Cahiers*. But even prose imposed difficulties on the young Gide. Although his prose style at the time was the envy of Louÿs, his inspiration depended too much on momentary fervor, with the result that, in the early journal, his admirable style appears only in detached fragments. He thus proved unable to work out satisfactorily any of the many projects in prose that he noted in his diary, such as *Allain* and *La Nouvelle Education sentimentale*. He finally contented himself with fusing some of them into *Les Cahiers*.

More or less conscious of his own failings and fearful that

a less alien outside world, with its familiar things and people, would impose upon him and distract him from an intimate communion with his feelings to the disadvantage of his work, Gide went into isolation, at the end of May, 1890, in order to write the great French novel.[11]

Au printemps je sentis le moment venu; mais, pour écrire mon livre, il me fallait la solitude. . . . Dans la complète solitude où je vécus, je pus chauffer à blanc ma ferveur, et me maintenir dans cet état de transport lyrique hors duquel j'estimais malséant d'écrire.[12]

It is true that all this is not unusual, being a common practice for creation in general, but in the light of what issued forth from this three-month retreat we have reason to be surprised. A novelist or poet may go into isolation to be alone with his imaginary world and to compose and work out perceptions gained from an intimate contact with life. But his contact is made prior to the period of isolation and is a result of the interplay between the artist and reality. He must bring something real to his isolation for it to be fruitful. Now Gide inadvertently combined these two processes. He withdrew in order to be alone with the subject matter of his book, which he thought was a real relationship with Madeleine. But, since this relationship was largely a construct of his imagination, he found he could not write the book he had projected. He had borne within him the novel whose axis was his love for about two or three years before writing a word. During that time his conception of Madeleine, as well as his love for her, became so stylized and intellectual that the feelings they evoked in him had lost whatever spontaneity and authenticity they may once have had. The direct and total perception of himself and Madeleine in relation to each other was an experience Gide never suggested until after Madeleine's death, and probably never had while she was alive.[13] Yet one would expect such a perception to be the foundation of, or at least implicit in, a book such as he had projected. Instead, he substituted the emotion deriving from the concept of his relationship. What occupied his mind and "alone dwelled in his heart" was not so much the book but the subject of his book: the fact of his loving someone, the fact of his own emotion. He was more concerned with the mechanisms within himself than with the interplay between himself and Madeleine. Even the poem he labored over for Louÿs indicates this obsession: his main interest is less with the object of his love than with "mieux choisir les mots pour le . . . dire."

Gide had withdrawn to Annecy to create a frame of mind facilitating the contemplation described by Schopenhauer and so necessary for a felicitous creative act. But, alone in his ivory tower, Gide proved able to contemplate only himself and his self-engendered emotions. The "state of lyrical ecstasy" itself became the bulk of the book, while Madeleine fell by the wayside, as though she were not necessary or even important. In short, Gide started off with a concept instead of a percept and isolated himself in the vain hope of recasting his conceptual experience into "visceral" percepts for which he had no real-life complement. His failure to realize his hopes will become clearer upon closer consideration of his first work.

Les Cahiers consist of two diaries: "Le Cahier blanc," which deals with "l'amour-souvenir," and "Le Cahier noir," which reveals the tragic demise of the intimist hero, André Walter. The first *Cahier* indirectly recounts the story of Walter's love for his cousin Emmanuèle, the separation imposed on them by André Walter's mother as she lay dying, Emmanuèle's marriage to T., and most important, Walter's idea to write a book immortalizing his eternal and everlasting love. In the second *Cahier*, Walter sets out to write his novel and draws up its plan. He registers in his diary the emotions evoked by the memories to be consecrated in his novel and struggles vainly against the temptation of the flesh while each submission to it exaggerates his ideal of purity. When news comes of Emmanuèle's death he is somewhat relieved, because with no physical existence to compete with his memory of her she lives only in his memory and thereby belongs chastely to him alone. As his memories grow more and more intense, her physical presence becomes more vivid until, by dint of evoking these hallucinations at will and too often, he becomes dominated by them and ultimately dies of brain fever with the purity-fixation on his mind: "how white the snow is. . . . They say one can have beautiful dreams in it. The snow is pure." [14] Shortly after this entry, Walter is found dead in the snow, some distance away from his cottage. The whole episode lasts about eight months, the first entry being supposedly made late in March or early April, 1889, and the last during the final weeks of November of that same year.

The narrative itself is practically nonexistent, since *Les Cahiers* are in diary form and trace only the protagonist's thoughts, emotions, memories. The protagonist, like his double André Gide, withdrew into solitude in order to write a book consecrating his love for Emmanuèle. This we learn near the end of the first notebook. But soon after we find that Walter's plans are inconsistent. At the beginning of the "Cahier noir," he draws up a plan for *Allain,* and formulates its aesthetic theories. Thus, Walter's work, like Gide's, is to be reduced to a single character; "un personnage seulement, et encore un quelconque, ou plutôt son cerveau, n'est que le lieu commun où le drame se livre, le champ clos où les adversaires s'assaillent." [15] The adversaries are "l'Ange et la Bête," the Angel and the Brute, and their battlefield is the person of Allain; each is to assume his proper guise, body and soul, and the entire proceedings are to be recorded in the form of a novel. Here, too, Emmanuèle is relegated to a minor role. But Walter suggests an awareness of his inconsistency. "Pour l'ange," he says later in the plan for *Allain*, "le désir toujours plus grand de monter; il lui faut un but, et qu'il y tende: c'est vers toi, Emmanuèle, idéalement supérieure. (Et là, tout le roman impossible.)" [16] Here Walter states what Gide could not admit before, his inability to write of Emmanuèle.

This brief description of *Les Cahiers d'André Walter* is sufficient to indicate some of its grave faults. Gide himself suggests several in *Si le Grain ne meurt* and elsewhere: the "ejaculatory" tone, lack of precise vocabulary, the too special subject, complacency, and above all, unfamiliarity with the possibilities of the French language.[17] Jean Hytier notices still further and more pivotal flaws. *Les Cahiers d'André Walter*, he says, violate the laws of poetic treatment and aesthetic composition by showing great hesitation in regard to "the intimate harmony of details with the themes" and to "the hierarchy of elements." Moreover, the poetry of the notebooks "does not adapt itself to such conflicts," and the struggle therein described is too internal to sustain drama.[18]

The absence of order, or composition, and the too great diversification of material in this first attempt can be accounted for by young Gide's eagerness to pour his whole life, its full twenty years of fervor and anguish, joy and sadness, mysticism and rationalism, into this *magnum opus*. One might add that he was especially conscious of sounding the responsive chord, of speaking, as Goethe did in his *Leiden des jungen Werthers*, for an entire generation.

Of significance, too, is the conception itself of *Les Cahiers*. Granted that the notion of publishing journals was not new to Gide,[19] still, the fact that he chose the journal form for his first work can again be seen as the result of his difficulties with reality. For the book that he had long projected, entitled *La Nouvelle Education sentimentale*, of which only a fragment was published in the *Oeuvres complètes*,[20] or *Allain*, which never saw publication, was apparently intended, at first, to be something quite unlike the final result, *Les Cahiers*. Gide hints at his original intentions in *Notes d'un voyage en Bretagne*:

> Pendant le retour, j'ai senti ce trouble étrange qui précède la création; je voyais de nouveau, comme parfois, des lambeaux de l'histoire d'*Alain*, ou de l'*Education*, qui s'éclairaient subitement d'un grand jour.[21]

This passage is enlightening on two accounts. First, the hesitation between two titles for the same subject matter indicates that, by 1889, Gide had in mind just one book. Secondly, the use of the term "histoire" to describe this book sheds light on his original conception of the work. However slight the evidence brought forth by the term may be, it is nevertheless significant that it can be made to apply only with great difficulty to the final result. The plan of *Les Cahiers*, we learn at the beginning of the second notebook, is to reduce the narrative element to its essentials, excluding all that is exterior to the intimate drama. In the body of the notebooks, too, the "story" is barely implied, its bulk consisting almost entirely of the musings and emotional outbursts of the protagonist. Though discreetly suggesting a "story," the author of the journals is not primarily concerned with the narration of events as the word "histoire" implies.

The fragment of *La Nouvelle Education sentimentale* presents more substantial evidence suggesting that Gide radically changed the conception of his first book. The choice of a Flaubertian model is itself indicative of his original plan. It is true, as Jean Delay points out,[22] that Gide felt many affinities with Frédéric Moreau. But more than Flaubert's hero or the subject matter of *L'Education sentimentale*, it was the artistry of his compatriot that enchanted Gide and that he would have liked to imitate. The style of the fragment resembles a pastiche of Flaubert, employing the cadence, the harmony, and the imperfect tenses so dear to him. Gide's success in imitating the master seemed assured but for two stumbling blocks: his understandable desire to be original and, more significant, the third-person narrative device. The fragment is one of the few cases in which Gide uses this traditional narrative technique.

The fact that this technique is rare in Gide's fiction, that it appears in a fragment of an abandoned first work, and that the final result of the same long gestation period was the two notebooks of *Les Cahiers d'André Walter*, all seem to indicate that Gide first intended to write a traditional novel using the third-person narrative, failed to realize his intentions, and published, instead, the journal of an imaginary figure. The publication of private journals had been in vogue long before *Les Cahiers d'André Walter*; Sainte-Beuve, for example, used the device of publishing works of fictitious authors with his *Vie, poésies, et pensées de Joseph Delorme* (1829). But fiction in the form of journals was somewhat of an innovation in French literature. If we consider for a moment some of the implications of using the third-person narrative, we shall be more able to understand why Gide abandoned his original plans.

Essential to the discussion of fictional technique is the relationship between the narrator and the narrative. This relationship is determined in the main by whether the story is told in the first or the third person. Percy Lubbock formulates this relationship as "point of view" and sees it as governing "the whole intricate question of method, in the craft of fiction." [23] Now the viewpoint of the omniscient author exacts precisely what Gide found it difficult to accomplish, the close and objective scrutiny of reality. This scrutiny is essential to the third-person narrative because the author observes the actions of his characters *in vivo* and from without. That is, he must observe and depict his characters acting and fulfilling their destiny in an external context resembling reality, or, at least, an analogous cosmic system. In a first-person narrative, however, the importance of external reality can be greatly diminished, since the narrator is free to reduce the external world to his own dimensions and needs. This is especially the case where the narrator is the protagonist, where the main concern is the expression of his own emotions, and where the emphasis on external reality can be replaced by his subjective reactions to it. Here were the advantages of the first-person narrative that offered Gide a way out of the dilemma posed by the need to observe a reality from which he felt dissociated. The first-person device, or more accurately, the diary form, enabled him to sustain a tone and intensity of expression impossible in the third person. The fragment of *La Nouvelle Éducation sentimentale* succeeds admirably in evoking a mood; but to do so it necessitated an intimate observation of the real world and the pose of observer that Gide was happily able to effect for a moment, in the fragment, but that he was unable to sustain. Thus we have merely a fragment of a novel Gide projected in the traditional form. Like Edouard, in *Les Faux-Monnayeurs,* André Walter could have said of his book:

> si je ne parviens pas à l'écrire, ce livre, c'est que l'histoire du livre m'aura plus intéressé que le livre lui-même; qu'elle aura pris sa place; et ce sera tant mieux.[24]

Gide later realized the bane of the *intimiste* and remarked upon the bad effects his restricted vision had upon *Les Cahiers.*

> La préoccupation où je vivais avait ce grave inconvénient d'absorber introspectivement toutes mes facultés atten-

tives; je n'écrivais et ne souhaitais rien écrire que d'intime.[25]

Thus limited to the inner side of consciousness and willing this limitation, Gide poured his whole soul into his first book; all was supposedly to revolve around his love for Madeleine. But she disappears and his love for her gives way to the entire range of his emotions, regardless of their stimuli. The introspective absorption of all his attentiveness left him without a point of reference by which he might have better organized and cogently simplified the expression of his emotions into a complex yet ordered whole. The disorganized complexity of *Les Cahiers d'André Walter*, due to Gide's desire to compose a *summa* of his youth, tends to muddle clarity and diversify materials. There results what Gide was to describe in 1897 as the expression of an impassioned stupefaction.[26] Not all the elements included, moreover, were consciously controlled by the young author; indeed, as he admits in his memoirs, he even strove for vagueness and mystery, thereby covering up lacunae of knowledge or emotion with vague words or fantasies.

Gide himself saw the book as a dramatization of the dire effects resulting from the separation of body and soul. "With much love, music, metaphysics, and poetry, this was the subject of my book." [27] Needless to say, this understanding of the book was not universally shared by the critics of the time. Most offered different interpretations of the book and of the causes of Walter's madness and subsequent death. Some attributed his trouble to a new "mal du siècle," others, to the struggle between his intelligence and his will, between introspection and action, or to various other elements of his being, all in conflict with one another.[28] Most seemed to approve of the book; Mallarmé saw it as "the sweetest veil drawn over a phase of youth now dead," [29] Maeterlinck, as a "sad and marvelous breviary of Virgins," and felt that "le mal" elaborated in *Les Cahiers* was indicative of something either in the air or in the nature of man.[30]

However scantily Gide sketches Walter, he nevertheless suggests a number of conflicts which precipitate Walter's intensity and, finally, his death. Walter is caught in the struggle not only between body and soul, but between religion and art, dream and reality, love and desire, morality and instinct, and many more apparent dichotomies.[31] Moreover, since Walter is involved—as was Gide—in writing a book commemorating and keeping alive his love, problems of an aesthetic nature, art versus time and art versus reality, necessarily enter within the scope of the book. Indeed, the personality indicated by Gide is complex and his problems are varied. But the true subject of *Les Cahiers* is Gide's own vague and intense feelings, and its basic problem, communication of his intensity.

Gide frequently alludes to the difficulties of communication in *Les Cahiers* and in an entry to his "Cahier de notes de lectures" of July and August, 1890, suggests a possible solution. Commenting upon the style of Marie Bashkirtseff's *Journal*, he wrote:

> c'est évident qu'on ne peut jamais faire arriver à éprouver aux autres l'émotion sienne dans son intensité, qu'il vaut bien mieux en prendre son parti dès l'abord et par le talent insinuer l'émotion—la faire sentir symboliquement—sug-gestivement.[32]

In *Les Cahiers*, Gide attempted to follow these aesthetic principles. He hoped to "insinuate" emotion by skillfully arranging and composing his materials. But these materials changed as the pretexts for emotion changed. So long as Walter's hopes of uniting his soul with Emmanuèle's in platonic matrimony remained alive, he had an outlet for his emotions by and through their relationship. When Emmanuèle dies, near the beginning of the second notebook, this outlet is shut off. No longer a stabilizing influence from without, she becomes instead an object of his imagination entirely dependent upon him for existence. With both his mother and beloved dead, his ties, however tenuous, to the real world are severed and he is free to roam the inner side of consciousness. Thus he induces hallucinations which ultimately cause his death from brain fever. His memories, then, play a minor role in the second notebook; the major one is given to the preoccupations and activities of his life in seclusion. The materials, or pretexts, of "Le Cahier noir" are thus different from those of "Le Cahier blanc."

Walter's memories of his relationship with Emmanuèle, recalled when he has lost her to T., evoke intense emotions in him. Understanding that the full impact upon the reader of Walter's recollections and attendant emotions would be lost if he merely transcribed them, Gide prepared well in advance the first of such recollections.[33] By slowly building up emotional tension he hoped to evoke and suggest Walter's feelings in their full intensity.

The recollection itself consists of the first revelation of intimacy and sympathy between Walter and Emmanuèle. The fact that this memory is the first in the body of the book, that it is so definite and explicitly recalled, and that it was anticipated with all the love and affection of a first successful seduction, all make of it something special and of extreme importance. Scrutinizing his past, Walter thinks of the beginning of his relationship with Emmanuèle; but no mention is made of her, nor is anything more explicitly stated than:

l'éducation d'une âme; la former à soi—une âme aimante, aimée, semblable à soi pour qu'elle vous comprenne, et de si loin que rien ne puisse entre les deux qui les sépare.[34]

This entry is immediately followed by another discreet allusion to Emmanuèle; "Nous apprenions tout ensemble; je n'imaginais de joies qu'avec toi partagées." The books they read together are carefully mentioned, favorite passages are quoted. There follows a brief dictionary definition of the Greek word *sympathein* ("souffrir ensemble, se passionner ensemble"), which is the key to Walter's feelings towards his cousin and the point of this first section. For their intimacy, from Walter's point of view, at least, is based on the coincidence of enthusiasm. Thus, inevitably, a third element, frequently taken from literature, is required to prompt his feelings for Emmanuèle. A lull in these recollections is filled by plans for *Allain*, only to be terminated suddenly by the following:

le grand frisson, à la fois moral et physique, qui vous secoue au spectacle des choses sublimes, et que chacun de nous croyait seul avoir, de sorte qu'il n'en parlait pas à l'autre,—quelle joie quand nous le découvrîmes l'un chez l'autre pareil: ce fut une grande émotion.

The discovery that each experienced a similar "grand frisson" and the "grande émotion" that resulted form the substance of Walter's first detailed recollection.

"One summer evening we were returning from H***." The narrative begins in plain, even banal, terms. But since the episode has been prepared at least seven pages in advance and is thus informed, the understated narrative gains in evocative force. On the way back from a trip the two are left alone in a wagon for some time. They read the Bible together, pray silently, and when André begins to recite a poem he is surprised and moved because Emmanuèle picks it up and continues for several more lines.

> Et tous deux, comme il se faisait tard, nous sommes endormis, songeurs, pressés l'un contre l'autre, les mains jointes.

Again at home and despite the general joviality of the rest of the family, "we both preserved in our souls the memory of a more secret intimacy."

The evocative strength of the passage lies in the fact that it is an understated demonstration of the expository passages preceding it. Emmanuèle's name is specifically mentioned whereas previously she is indirectly alluded to. The intertwined recitation of a favorite poem combined with the evocative force of the poem itself, the pious prayer in silence, the innocent nap under a single shawl, all in the setting of an otherwise uneventful and banal trip described in detail, suggest the communion of souls through "sympathy."

Thus Gide prepared the explosion of the first recollection. Thereafter, any hint of sympathy between the two is immediately informed, invested with the emotions suggested here. The catalyst that precipitates his emotions and possibly similar ones in the reader, differs, but the process is the same. On one occasion direct physical contact (Emmanuèle's cool hand on his brow), initiates the diarist's emotions; even here, moreover, the original intermediary was art, Walter's rendition of Robert Schumann's *Novelettes*.[35] On another occasion it is the death of a child [36] or the alternating recitation of Baudelaire's "Recueillement." [37] No longer requiring the same painstaking and detailed preparation, the subsequent recollections of emotion become mere suggestions, briefly outlined: a phrase from "Recueillement," [38] a breeze that recalls Emmanuèle's caress,[39]

Emmanuèle reading over his shoulder,[40] are all evocations of prior events but intensified by the "sympathy" inherent in them as well as by the emotions Walter felt when they occurred.

The method outlined above is successful in one or two isolated instances. But frequent use to evoke the same vague emotion, "le grand frisson," without any shading, results in monotony. Moreover, the individuality latent in the various memories or pretexts for the evocation of sentiment is greatly undermined by the monotonous repetition of Walter's "grande émotion." No exchange of value between a pretext and the emotion evoked in Walter is ever apparent, though much of poetry's evocative power and precision lies in this exchange, in the "intimate harmony of details with the themes." [41] For example, at the deathbed of a small child, it is Emmanuèle's sadness that stirs his emotions; but no hint of compassion for the family of the deceased or of appreciation for Emmanuèle's compassion mars the intensity of Walter's feelings. Even the joy of sympathy is absent. "I hardly attended to anything but her, doing my best to act so that a smile would reward me," [42] Walter states blandly. He is moved by Emmanuèle's expressed feelings but in no way takes into account the nature or cause of these feelings. The recollected event thus loses importance and sheds no light upon what Walter himself felt.

In *Les Cahiers* the use of recollection for the communication of sentiment thus comes to a dead end because of repetition. Since the memories themselves retain little or no intrinsic value, they quickly lose any evocative force and their purpose and relevancy become obscure. Similarly the emotions they are to convey remain vague and through excessive use of the memory device are affirmed rather than evoked. Since the prime sentiment in Walter and Emmanuèle's relationship is sympathy, the simultaneity of feeling evoked, not by each other, but by some third element, Gide is forced to insert such catalysts too frequently. Thus there appear innumerable quotations from literature and allusions to composers. "For this reason we so enjoyed quoting the poets, not because we experienced emotion through them, but because, above all else, they recalled so much!" Thus, the quotations, too, lose their intrinsic value. "For it was not the word alone; for us, it had its legend, and the same one," [43] a personal legend of which the reader can never be sure. There arises, as well, a confusion in the mind of the reader between the evocative force a familiar quotation has for him and what it evoked in Emmanuèle and Walter. It appears as though Gide used the symbol of a renowned poet's emotion, for example, Baudelaire in "Recueillement," as a symbol of the emotions his protagonist felt. The relationship between Baudelaire's emotion and Walter's, if there be any, remains vague and arbitrary. It is probably true, despite Walter's denial, that Gide was trying to characterize Walter's emotions by means of famous quotations and that he was willing, as Pierre Louÿs suggested in a letter to Gide, to profit from the success of other artists. Louÿs' letter was not very encouraging for Gide, struggling with his book alone in his chalet, yet it carries some weight and validity:

> it is impossible that [your book] fail. I believe it will be extraordinary in its intimacy, in its monologue, in its personal life! Even if the character is unreal, you will have inserted details, trifles, phrases which are those of all men. . . . Baudelaire's verse, for example; your idea is charming. Everyone who knows the line will love you for having quoted it like that. [44]

It becomes apparent that by his use of selected memories Gide tried to narrow the concept of Walter's love to specific instances of its expression. In this way he hoped to make his hero's passion highly perceptible. But his success, we have seen, was limited. In the second notebook the problem of communication severely changes because of the "heroine's" death. Gide was thus obliged to find new means of expression.

II

The Symbol: Practice and Theory

It has been said that all of Gide is implicit in *Les Cahiers
d'André Walter*. For the most part one cannot question this
observation, especially in the light of the large amount of
autobiographical material Gide was to publish subsequently
and recent research on his formative years. Though his attitudes changed as he grew older, many of the problems he
touches upon in *Les Cahiers* remained with him long after
the death of his adolescent hero. From an aesthetic point of
view, however, the value of this observation is debatable.
Gide's later writings are generally quite simplified. The con-
stituent parts of each work are subordinated to its central idea;
complexity and confusion yield to simplification, to the point
of understating any given emotion or idea; diversification,
to tightly knit aesthetic organisms revolving about a single
theme. Thus limiting the thematic range of each book, Gide
was able to exploit more fully the complexities of a single
emotion or thought.

And yet in 1930 Gide had *Les Cahiers* republished, with some
mortification, to be sure, but also with the pride of having
gone beyond the errors he had made there. It is in this spirit
that he wrote the preface to the definitive edition of *Les
Cahiers* (1930). Except for a brief, final relapse in 1891, which
yielded *Les Poésies d'André Walter*, *Les Cahiers* purged Gide
of many of his aesthetically unsound tendencies. Just as he

rid himself of Walterism by "writing" it, he rid himself of the bad habits of the romantics, the mystics, and the intimists in the same way. The *Cahiers* are offered as an example of what not to do. Like Goethe, affixing to a later edition of *Werther* a similar admonition to the reader, Gide counsels in his preface "that a too impressionable young reader not seek here models of writing, feeling, or thinking."

The key to the lesson learned from the errors in *Les Cahiers* is stated in the same preface:

> at that age I did not know how to write and, perhaps precisely because I felt I had new things to say, I groped. I tried to subjugate language. I had not yet understood how much more one learns by submitting to it, and how instructive are those rules which are annoying at first, against which the mind rebels and which it wishes to reject.[1]

The lesson is simply that the artist, by abdicating his need to express his own emotions, does not necessarily produce a cold work of art, that respect for rules of grammar and composition need not cramp the creative process, and, as Gide was to repeat so frequently in his subsequent critical writings, the greater the formal obstacles, the surer the art that overcomes them. He applied to problems of aesthetics, in short, the wisdom of Jesus: who sacrifices himself in this world will be infinitely rewarded in the other. "Worry only about form," he advises the young writer in *Caractères*; "emotion will occupy it quite naturally. A perfect dwelling always finds a tenant." [2] This passage and the one following it, which restates his emphasis on artistic form, were first published in 1925, when he had already evolved for himself, and put into practice, his basic aesthetic principles. Yet he had suggested similar ideas long before, in his second published work, *Le Traité du Narcisse*, with the subtitle, *Théorie du symbole*.

In many ways *Les Cahiers* points to *Le Traité*, not only by virtue of the technical progress this latter work represents, but also by the concept of the work of art in the outline for *Allain* that Gide appended to "Le Cahier noir." The nature of the symbol changes, however, from a vehicle for personal emotion to one for objective truth.

Generally speaking, the term "symbol" is understood to mean a visible sign of an idea or quality with which it has something in common because of natural association or convention. In addition a symbol evokes something that cannot be realized in the mind of the reader by any other method. It conjures up what is not readily perceivable in the everyday world. The symbol thus implies the existence of things perceived by intuition, that is, beyond or above the ordinary range of the human mind. Like the metaphor it has a practical function, but it is not so much one of "presenting the notion in the most intelligible or convincing or arresting way" [3] as it is of evoking the notion in its most complete and total form. "A symbol is indeed the only possible expression of some invisible essence, a transparent lamp about a spiritual flame," [4] Yeats tells us in an essay on Blake.

The symbol is especially important as an aesthetic device because it presupposes a particular position vis-à-vis reality. For if the artist is interested in the immediate perception of the world as it is and for itself, if his interest is in the sensations caused by things around him, his need for symbols is greatly reduced; he presents the world as it appears to him, the faithful representation of that world as it is being his main object. [5] If, however, the artist does not consider the objects about him as ends in themselves, if he perceives something beyond that orders and interprets them, gives them universal meaning, then he is inevitably concerned with "that which stands for or represents something else." His observation of the world is an attempt to see a reason and order hidden under the welter of daily life. This is the mystical pose par excellence vis-à-vis reality. He chooses to tell the story of one family, one man, one episode, because he sees his particular subject as representative of some deeper truth. The subject of his work, then, is not an end in itself but a vehicle for some more general or universal notion. In such cases the work of art is the arena in which a given theme is expressed by means of appropriate pretexts. Thus, in many works of art the pretext is a vehicle of some metaphorical relationship, resembling a symbol.

There exists, then, for the artist who employs symbols, an intangible realm beyond the immediate world. Like the prophet, he has the gift to see through and interpret contingent phenomena. With his sensitivity and feelings as guides, he expresses his insights in a form accessible to those primarily preoccupied with the daily needs of living. Gide's natural frame of mind since early adolescence was precisely one which is given to interpreting and creating a symbolic art. His dissociation from reality, his long familiarity with the Bible and biblical exegesis, augmented and sustained by his introspection and a natural tendency to suppose the clandestine, made him extremely conscious that "we see through a glass darkly" and that only the things we do not see are eternal. He saw the world as a riddle to be solved, and passing phenomena as signs representing permanent forms of each species.

When he read Schopenhauer during his eighteenth year Gide found formulated many of the ideas he had been nurturing. The German philosopher's insistence upon a true reality of the Idea and the gift of genius to perceive and express it encouraged Gide along his aesthetic and mystical path. Furthermore, in distinguishing history from poetry, the behavior of men from that of a single man, Schopenhauer encouraged Gide's self-scrutiny. The historian can never know his subject as well as the poet his. "The poet . . . has comprehended the Idea of man from some definite side which is to be represented; thus it is the nature of his own self that objectifies itself in it for him." The poet, then, approaches the inner truth of all men. "He is the mirror of mankind, and brings to its consciousness what it feels and does." [6] For the revelation of the Idea, Schopenhauer sanctions the use of imagery and, somewhat reluctantly, the use of symbols and other tropes.[7]

In *Les Cahiers d'André Walter*, Gide suggests similar ideas. For him, as for Schopenhauer, phenomena are the passing, contingent forms of some eternal and immutable truth, an Idea that each one tries to manifest. They are signs, a divine language that only the intuitive mind can comprehend; that is, only through the will-less perception of reality can we intuit and contemplate the truths that lie beyond the transient multitudes. Thus Walter repudiates reason because it is voluntary and authoritative; it restricts the receptivity of the poet's soul and hinders the complete fulfillment of his duty to manifest those truths within him. Life, he states, is not an end but a means for the expression of truths. "We live in order to manifest but often do so involuntarily, unconsciously, and for truths which we do not know; for we are ignorant of our very reasons for existence." [8] The true poet, we are reminded by Schopenhauer, is the mirror of mankind and thus "all that has ever moved a human heart, all that human nature in any situation has ever produced from itself" [9] find expression in his emotions. Precisely because they are universal, his feelings make up the truths, the Ideas, concerning man and his situation that he is called upon to manifest.

But are these notions beyond expression? André Walter

acknowledges the difficulty involved in translating visions and emotions into words; like most poets he bewails the inadequacy of language.

> What a child I was to believe that everything can be said!
> Even if it were so, the words themselves would not exist.
> Language is only for ordinary feelings; extreme emotions
> evade the effort to reveal them.[10]

The mere existence of *Les Cahiers* indicates that Gide did not consider language totally incapable of conveying his emotions. Yet the assertion that there are no words intense enough to evoke them faithfully has a double effect. First, because he does attempt to convey emotion, when he succeeds we are invited to consider the emotion conveyed, however intense, as understated and a modest approximation. In this way, the author's emotions are intensified literally beyond imagination. Secondly, because words are lacking or inadequate, we are urged to recognize other expressive devices, such as the recollections and literary quotations used symbolically in *Les Cahiers*. Still another device, especially prevalent in "Le Cahier noir," is the detail or image turned symbol.

The predominant images of the second notebook are taken from music. This is not surprising since Walter would have preferred to write not in French but in music.[11] Music appealed to him precisely because of its lack of semantic precision; its power to evoke pure and undelineated emotion, which is too easily profaned by words and rhetoric. Moreover, music is traditionally the language of the soul and of angels. Thus a key image and the most intricately prepared symbol of *Les Cahiers* is the dissonant snapping of a piano string. In what is the most lyrical passage of the book Gide manages to reproduce the resonance and reverberations of the broken string.

Je jouais—et le piano surmené frémissait de toutes ses cordes; mais, à trop vibrer, soudain, une s'est rompue.—Je m'arrêtai tremblant à l'incisif éclat de cette corde métallique.—Elle s'est tue, mais comme une onde harmonieuse ondulant sur tous les degrés, longtemps ont répondu, douloureusement émues, les plus lointaines harmoniques. Puis l'onde aérienne soulevée s'est épandue plus subtile.— Tout se rendort. Le silence un instant déchiré se referme, qui m'enveloppe de peur et de ma solitude.[12]

Profoundly and mysteriously disturbed by this incident, Walter is unable to continue playing, to read, or to plunge himself into reverie. Even while he writes his journal, "over and over in the night [he] still hears a sob—the string of a lute which breaks." The profound significance of this midnight episode is only partially clarified by the rest of the journal entry. Following immediately upon the variant of the main image ("la corde d'un luth qui se brise") appears an apparently unrelated quotation: *"Etant environnés d'une si grande nuée de témoins."* [13] In an effort to further convey his emotion, Walter takes the biblical verse as a point of departure, trying to recast it first metaphorically and then symbolically. After entreating his readers to a more active faith by reminding them of the great heroes of the past, whom he calls "witnesses," the author of Hebrews continues on the last lap of his epistle in the following manner:

> Wherefore seeing we also are compassed about with so great a cloud of witnesses, let us lay aside every weight, and the sin which doth so easily beset us.[14]

These past heroes form a vast host watching the progress of those yet on earth. It is precisely this image that strikes another responsive chord in André Walter and that he tries to render in the two styles. The first rendition is metaphorical and in the manner of Victor Hugo.

MÉTAPHORIQUE; HUGO.

D'invisibles clartés flottent autour de nous, dans ce que nous croyons la nuit noire; les âmes luisent comme des cierges, les âmes mortes déjà ou qui ne sont pas encore nées; l'immatériel espace frissonne de lumières—et l'homme est entouré de légions infinies qui s'échelonnent jusqu'à Dieu.

The point of view is terrestrial, with man at the center of the scene. *"D'invisibles clartés"* is an antithesis typical of Hugo, the arch-Romantic; so, too, are the useless words in the phrase *"dans ce que nous croyons la nuit noire."* What grates particularly on Walter's sensitivity is the clarity of the scene and, paradoxically, the too frequent intrusions, implied or real, of the first person. The symbolic rendition, on the other hand, is succinct, understated, and transcendental: *"Sur champ d'azur, de grands anges penchés qui contemplent."* [15] This fragment is the whole variation. Using the terminology of heraldry, which employs colors and charges in a symbolic way, Walter describes an imaginary coat of arms that relates with particular aptness to his own self-image. The presence of angels, rare in heraldry, suggests his aspirations to purity, his angelism. But one may go further in heraldic analysis because of the specified posture of the angels. They are deep in contemplation; but because they are also "penchés," their vision must have a direction and object. In this pose, they recall the "cloud of witnesses" in Hebrews XII: 1. Moreover, if in heraldry a coat of arms is an identification and if Walter truly felt himself "compassed about with" witnessing souls, then it would not be unreasonable to conclude that *he* is the object of their contemplation.

Walter must have felt himself precisely at the focus of these angels' attention when he reacted so violently to the snapping piano-string. For he returns to the problem of spiritual and emotional resonance, declaring that the vibrations of the soul are most probably subject to the same or similar mathematical laws that govern physical resonance. "The trembling of a single [soul] immediately moves all those around it that are capable of complete unison." This discussion calls our attention to a similar one in an earlier entry:

> La moindre vibration d'une âme agite longtemps les espaces autour d'elle; les moindres cris éveillent des retentissements très lointains. On n'altère pas impunément les rapports mystérieux des êtres; rien ne s'éteint. . . . C'est le refrain de quelque premier chant d'extase qui m'emporte ainsi l'âme vers des adorations inconnues.[16]

The association between the broken piano string and the New Testament verse thus becomes a bit clearer. In addition to the timelessness evoked both by the biblical quotation and the study of spiritual resonances, there is a connection subtly established between the vast host of witnesses watching Walter and the broken piano string become a sob, or "la corde d'un luth qui se brise." For just as souls eternally envelop us like a cloud, so too their sobs, or vibrations, which are never spent, can strike the responsive (i.e., chosen) heart of the living.

> Et c'est ce qui fait que parfois nous nous sentons émus de mystérieuses tendresses: c'est qu'un accord épars dans l'air aura fait frissonner notre âme; un chant subtil, imperceptible, en elle aura éveillé quelque allitération latente.[17]

The reverberating sound of the broken piano string, we can conclude, was to Walter's agitated mind the materialized sob of an observing soul. But this only partially clarifies Walter's deep reaction to it. In a state of near hallucination[18] Walter must have seen in the snapping cord an event of personal significance. Not only did he feel that the sob originated from one of the witnessing souls but also that the witness was Emmanuèle herself. For hers was indeed the only soul to whose resonance he was completely attuned; the repeated meditations on *sympathein* have as their object precisely the accord he felt between their souls. Emmanuèle dies, we learn in a footnote, on July 31, nearly a month before the piano-string episode. But just one mention of her death is made during this period, and that in reference to the love intrigue of *Allain*.[19] Although he is able to maintain his journal, the absence of any allusion to her death suggests a willful suppression of this painful event. The entry he made earlier in the evening of this key episode further suggests that he suppressed his reaction to her death. Here, as though simultaneously talking and not talking about Emmanuèle, he discusses the formal techniques of expressing emotion. In a close analysis of the last two lines of Verlaine's "Mon Rêve familier,"

> Et pour sa voix lointaine, et calme, et grave, elle a
> L'inflexion des voix chères qui se sont tues,

which undoubtedly evoke Emmanuèle in his mind, he concerns himself only with their sonorous or rhythmical qualities. Thus it is significant that a few hours later he should use a funeral metaphor to describe the reverberations of the dead chord. "I remained trembling at the mute keyboard, afraid I might again provoke mourning for the defunct note." Here the idea of death inadvertently rises to the surface of Walter's consciousness, and particularly the idea of Emmanuèle's death.

47

Profoundly shaken by the sound of the piano string, he is afraid to continue playing and to risk reactivating its mournful tones. To give in to his mourning he would risk losing himself in a flood of uncontrollable emotion. So he diverts his attention from his own feelings by composing variations on a biblical quotation; and yet this same quotation serves as an explanation as well as a conscious control of the deep impact caused by the episode.

The breaking piano string thus forced Walter to an awareness of Emmanuèle's death and of her constant spiritual presence, fused with the emotions evoked by this awareness. This is one of the few things happening to Walter over which he had no control. Most of the events in the notebooks have their source in the intimate and internal drama of Walter's life; the recollections of his youth, the books he read, favorite quotations, the struggle between body and soul, even Emmanuèle herself are all materials directly dependent upon himself and subject to his conscious artistic control. But if the event had symbolic value for Walter it was a pure expressive symbol for Gide, a device he manipulated to precipitate Walter's emotions and to evoke similar emotions in the reader. Gide intended the event to function as a "pregnant situation," in Schopenhauer's words, in which a significant character discloses himself.[20] By taking a common or easily imagined experience and magnifying it with the perception and emotional intensity of his hero, Gide constructed an expressive symbol conveying Walter's feelings to the reader. Moreover, all the elements that give it symbolic value for Walter necessarily enter into its effectiveness as a literary symbol. The attentive reader, Gide hoped, would understand and appreciate at once the causes and nature of the emotions evoked.

The efficacy of the symbolic image lies in its power to force the willing reader into perceiving relationships between the intangible and the concrete. Discursive language lacks this power, Gide well knew, and for this reason he has Walter frequently complain of the inadequacy of language. Syntax, the inescapable relationship of subject, verb, and attribute, is inadequate to delineate perceived relationships that are subtle and tenuous. Forcing such subtle correlations into linguistic straitjackets tends to render them precise, it is true, but limits them as well to conceptual terms. What Walter wants to facilitate, on the other hand, is the reader's perception of the rapport between two disparate essences. He falls back on Verlaine:

> *Pas la couleur, rien que la nuance.*
> C'est alors dans le rapport des mots, non plus dans la phrase entière.[21]

In addition to the judicious use of the relationships between words and what they connote, Walter includes in this same discussion the evocative forces of sonority and rhythm. Thus, in aligning under the same heading the three principal features of poetic language (meaning, sound, and rhythm), he approaches Gide's conception of the symbol as we have seen it at work in *Les Cahiers*. The prime objective of both is the expression of emotion or idea in perceptual and not conceptual terms.

Even after the most careful reading one is tempted to question the *raison d'être* of *Les Cahiers;* Gide's insistence upon an intimate conflict between body and soul whose intensity can be shared only by a few immediately excludes the sympathy of most readers. And yet how could Gide have known that his intimate drama was extremely personal before he had written *Les Cahiers*, and before he had emerged from the cloistered atmosphere of his youth? Gide offers this same excuse in *Si le Grain ne meurt.*[22] But naiveté is only a partial explanation. The real justification may be found in *Les Cahiers* themselves and in Walter's determination to write.

After the news of Emmanuèle's death Walter found it difficult to recover from the shock; he was unable to write, to lose himself in reverie, or even to play the piano: "Silence, then; words are profane." [23] Finally, he begins to stir and finds in his proposed work a point of reorientation. This first becomes apparent in the sole entry of August 16, in a paraphrase of two verses from the Old Testament:

> *Et les sommets des montagnes reparurent.—*
> *Conduis-moi sur ce rocher où je ne puis*
> *atteindre.*[24]

The full significance of these lines is made clear immediately afterward by a Pauline verse: "L'oeuvre de chacun sera manifestée." [25] Spurred on by the need to manifest—to express himself—he awakens and begins to work.

At the basis of his aesthetic and ethical credo is the adage "il faut manifester." What one must manifest is one's own authentic self, for only in this way the truths of which we are ignorant are given palpable, concrete form. The true artist, or genius, achieves authenticity because in him the objectification of the will is complete. He thus approaches the Idea of man. He observes himself in an attempt to understand what is universal in his nature and in his actions. He recasts this material in a form "made more clear by the representation, and more significant by the arrangement." [26] Gide, we have seen, intended Walter to be representative of late-nineteenth-century French adolescence; his book was to represent certain crises of a typical youth. These were the crises that he felt called upon to manifest.

Thus Gide's first justification for *Les Cahiers d'André Walter* was that he thought them to be a true expression of the dilemmas of adolescence. Later, in his maturity, he saw them as strictly personal, yet important as a sincere biographical, if not universal, manifestation of his mystical youth.

Les Cahiers d'André Walter were finished and the proofs were read and corrected by the end of November, 1890. Shortly afterwards, by chance, Gide met the renowned Maurice Barrès at Perrin's, their common publisher's.[27] At this moment of his career Barrès was the champion of individualism and, by this token, one of Gide's heroes. The older writer had admired the page-proofs of *Les Cahiers* and decided to give its young author a helping hand. With no previous contact with the intellectual ferment of the 1880's, Gide plunged into the Parisian literary whirl. Barrès invited him to a banquet honoring the Symbolist poet Jean Moréas, which was attended by most of the eminent litterateurs of the day. One out of many attracted and held Gide's eye, Stéphane Mallarmé. *"Barrès introduces me to Mallarmé"*; Gide, as though entranced by the idea, reverently confided these underlined words to his *Agenda*.[28] He read Mallarmé for the first time and wrote an enthusiastic letter to Paul Valéry; he said that art does not stagnate, "il évolue en moi terriblement . . . [je] me postais moi-même comme apôtre de vérités neuves, (vérités d'art s'entend), de vérités antagonistes des vôtres. Je me savais symboliste infiniment. . . . Depuis, tout est changé. Mallarmé surtout en est cause." In addition, a special issue of the revue *La Plume*, dedicated to Jean Moréas, revealed the theories and faith of the Symbolists, all of which "me semblent une apologie directe de mon livre quand ce ne sont pas ses phrases propres décalquées. Donc," he concludes, "je suis symboliste et sachez-le." Despite the fact that he had produced only one slim volume, he enthusiastically claimed top billing in the movement. His domain, he decided, would be the novel, as poetry and drama were for Mallarmé and Maeterlinck respectively.[29] Although this was a presumptuous attitude, it proved to be a prophetic one; he soon fulfilled the role of chief theoretician for the novel. His second book, *Le Traité du Narcisse*, assured him of this position and established him as a bona fide Symbolist.

The *Traité*, as Jean Delay points out, appears to be less a theory of the novel than a symbol of a new ideal Gide began to formulate when he entered the literary circles of Paris. Up until this time he had lived, so he felt, in a relatively ordered universe. He was aware of his own turbulent nature, it is true, but basically he did not question his inherited religious view of the world, and his occasional waverings were only, apparently, like those of a rebellious child in moments of spite or stubbornness. All this changed when he came into contact with the Symbolists; he later described this, in his memoirs, as the most confused part of his life. These people were different from one another and from anything or anyone Gide had known; the group seemed to exteriorize his own internal chaos. Each voiced his own peculiar moral and aesthetic ideas, and most professed points of view diametrically opposed to the code Gide had been brought up with and still believed in. On the one hand, he found echoed many ideas he had long since assimilated: repudiation of the real world in favor of the absolute realms attainable only through art, belief in the divine mission of the artist, enthusiasm for the German romantics and idealists, and above all the exaltation of music as the end of poetry. On the other hand, his friends proclaimed all around him that wisdom begins only when one overcomes the fear of God and respect for established values. Gide was tremendously confused by this sudden exposure to the diversity of life and thought, whose existence he had hardly suspected before. The need for something stable, for some direction within by which to orient himself and order this new complexity, became essential if Gide was to evolve both emotionally and artistically. Seeing these new ideas exteriorized was one step in this direction, for in this way he was better able to gauge their value objectively. In weaker moments, and to these we owe the composition of *Les Poésies d'André Walter*, he even longed to return to the stability of Walterism. But he persevered; deliberately moving away from Walter he gradually developed a view of life contrary to the ecclesiastical concept of man and his role in the world. His propensity for religious exuberance and mysticism found an outlet instead in the aesthetic mysticism proclaimed by Mallarmé. Under the tutelage of Oscar Wilde he fashioned a pagan piety. "Perhaps that was true beauty, entirely physical," he says in a journal entry made while working on *Le Traité*. "My thinking," he continues further on in the same note, "is becoming voluptuously impious and pagan. I have to exaggerate that. I see now what I have to read: Stendhal, the Encyclopedia, Swift, Condillac . . . in order to dry out my heart. . . . And not worry about the rest. I have enough tears in me to irrigate thirty books." [30] Thus this new phase tended also to neutralize the emotional outbursts which, in *Les Cahiers*, Gide deemed the essence of poetry.

It was at this time too that he discovered the basic quality of the classics, modesty and its expressive analogue, litotes. [31] So, as he yielded to the French language, he yielded too to the genius of the ancients, and chose a classical symbol for his second work. These first acts of renunciation resulted in what Delay calls the first authentic expression of "Gidism."

Composing the *Traité* was apparently a difficult task; he complained in his correspondence with Valéry of the troubles and snares he encountered.

Still the effort spent in writing is not wasted, since it has clarified my entire aesthetics, ethics, and philosophy. And I won't be dissuaded from believing that each artist must have his own philosophy, ethics, and aesthetics. Without that, nothing can be created. The work of art is only a manifestation of it.[32]

This is precisely what we find in Gide's second work. In the long expository footnote, written at the same time as *Le Traité*, he flatly states the aesthetic and ethical implications of his theory.

> Les Vérités demeurent derrière les Formes-Symboles. Tout phénomène est le Symbole d'une Vérité. Son seul devoir est qu'il la manifeste. Son seul péché: qu'il se préfère.[33]

Not only ourselves but all that appears on earth is a symbol and thus must manifest the idea it conceals. The moral question is not whether an idea is good or bad but whether it is well represented. For all must be represented, whether scandalous or acceptable to society. The function of the artist, then, is to express faithfully the ideas he perceives, subordinating to this end the word, the sentence, indeed the entire work of art. But what does one manifest? One learns that in silence, Gide answers cryptically, suggesting that it is in silent contemplation that one learns what one is. To know what one must represent, then, involves knowing oneself; the key to this knowledge is sincerity and self-scrutiny.

The basic ethical formula of *Le Traité* repeats, it is true, the Walterian adage, "one must manifest." But although Walter manifested a personal struggle and its ensuing emotions, this struggle was an effort to conform to the inherited notions of the pure life. Gide's new theory also required that "we all represent," but one is to represent one's own standards of behavior or the struggle to find them in oneself.

Thus, his new ideal is not to be found in a priori formulae but in each man's inner potential for action.

The body of the essay revolves about the legendary figure of Narcissus. Gide uses Narcissus in his traditional pose as an image, his posture as symbolic. The series of imaginary vignettes that make up the treatise illustrate the ideas expounded in the footnote. The *Traité* is in three parts, with a prologue and epilogue. The prologue sets the scene and presents the central figure. Impelled by a desire to see himself, Narcissus sets out in search of a mirror and finds the river of time. But once at its edge, what appears is more than just his reflection. He sees flowers from the river banks, trunks of trees, bits of sky reflected in the water, a whole series of images diversified by the movement and flow of the current. No two images are the same, yet they are always the same forms that pass, differentiated only by the water's motion. This repetition can be explained, Narcissus reasons, if the forms that constantly recur are imperfect and are trying to attain perfection. The realm they seek, then, must be Paradise, the domain of perfection.

The description of Paradise and its loss as imagined or dreamed by Narcissus forms the first part of the triptych. Paradise is the Garden of Ideas, and contains them all, but because each form is perfect and archetypal they are few in number, and the Garden is therefore small. Androgynous Adam, alone and bored because his identity is only that of a forced spectator, decides to know himself by a gesture of self-affirmation. He breaks a twig off the tree of knowledge. Suddenly time and the world are born. Each pure object is transformed through the optics of time into multitudes, each imperfectly revealing its origin. The first part ends with man's efforts to recapture Paradise.

The shortest section of the book, Part II, places Narcissus in Paradise, making of him a pure Idea. But he has his back to the Garden; he sees vague and imperfect forms passing in front of him in the river of time. Were he to turn around, he would discern the realm of the pure Idea. But, instead, he chooses to contemplate their imperfect reflections in the water, much like the inhabitants of Plato's cavern. The theme of this panel is "Paradise always has to be reconstructed." The sin is always the same: self-preference. It is at this juncture that Gide inserts the long footnote. The panel ends by suggesting that Paradise could be regained if only we were attentive.

With this thought Gide takes us back to the ideas of contemplation and the Narcissistic posture. The Poet, we are told at the beginning of Part III, is he who, by contemplating, sees Paradise. Here, for the first time, Gide fuses the figure of Narcissus and the Poet and reveals the point of the work. Like the scientist and the scholar, the Poet observes and contemplates the objects of reality in the hope of reaching their essence, the archetype of specific phenomena. Unlike either, however, the Poet proceeds by intuition rather than by reason.

> Le poète pieux contemple; il se penche sur les symboles, et silencieux descend profondément au coeur des choses,— et quand il a perçu, visionnaire, l'Idée, l'intime Nombre harmonieux de son Etre, qui soutient la forme imparfaite, il la saisit, puis, insoucieux de cette forme transitoire qui la revêtait dans le temps, il sait lui redonner une forme éternelle, *sa* Forme véritable enfin, et fatale,—paradisiaque et cristalline.[34]

Thus the poet is more than Narcissus. He does more than contemplate and perceive "à demi-mot"; he creates as well. The work of art is a reconstruction of Paradise, or of the Absolute, and thus it exists beyond time. The goal of the poet, of course, is knowledge of the world about him. It is his function to perceive and give voice to this knowledge. But since it is a special kind of knowledge, one distinct from erudition, a special vocabulary is required for its expression and communication. This special vocabulary is composed of symbols and the symbolic attributes of language, rhythm, and sonority. *Le Traité du Narcisse* is at a pole diametrically opposed to *Les Cahiers*. Instead of being vague, fervent, and synthetic, it is precise, reserved, and analytic. Madeleine, responding to both a recent reading of the essay and a letter from Gide, reflected in her journal his underlying intentions. "It is certainly what you wanted to do—an exercise in artistic rhetoric." [35] Since he was dealing with an exercise in objective and analytic thinking clothed in an aesthetically appealing form, his main concern was the crystalline representation of his idea. The essay thus appears to follow the notes on the novel indicated in *Les Cahiers d'André Walter* more closely than do the *Cahiers* themselves. There, through Walter, Gide explained his theories:

> Non point une vérité de réalisme, contingente fatalement; mais une vérité théorique, absolue (du moins humainement). Idéale, oui! Comme définit Taine: idéale, c'est-à-dire où l'idée apparaisse toute pure. Il faut la faire saillir de l'oeuvre. C'est une démonstration.

Further on Walter states, "un roman c'est un théorème." [36] If we take "théorème" to mean a proposition whose validity is made evident through demonstration, then Walter's statements apply with particular cogency to the structure of *Le Traité*. We see, then, the expository footnote of *Le Traité* as the theoretical truth, the proposition made evident by its demonstration in the body of the essay.

The theoretical truth, Platonic in nature, behind *Le Traité* is that every phenomenon is a form-symbol of some truth, and as such bears some vestigial recollection of the truth it symbolizes. Because each phenomenon is an ephemeral form of a truth, its only utility would be to express this truth, to subordinate itself to its free expression. Otherwise it would be useless, hence bad. Similarly the moral man, and the true artist is the moral man par excellence, sacrifices himself in order to realize his innate propensity for truth. He achieves this goal by contemplating himself in and among the objects of reality. The danger to be avoided is self-preference, which inhibits representation.

Thus forsaking the self-complacency of *Les Cahiers*, Gide crystallized an eternal truth perceived in the world about him in a work of art. The form given this Idea is the classical figure of Narcissus. Gide does not retell or interpret the legend, nor is he in fact interested in its narrative. He merely uses the image of Narcissus in his traditional posture as a symbol. Many critics, including Delay, have missed this important detail and have remarked the absence of Echo and indeed of the female in Gide's version of the legend. But it is not a version of the legend, and Echo has no more place in Gide's work than does Nemesis, who reputedly caused Narcissus to fall in love with his own reflection. Gide was intent on demonstrating his own proposition and took from his source only what was, in his view, pertinent to this demonstration. Gide's Narcissus, moreover, is a distillation of the classic figure; he incorporates no more than the eternal Narcissistic action. This action is, of course, self-contemplation maintained in the hope of ultimate physical possession of his reflection, and sharpened by the frustrating certainty of losing all at the moment of physical contact.

Narcissus, then, is a symbol representing a form of contemplation as well as the temptations inherent in this contemplation. We see him again in his traditional pose at the very end of the *Traité* when, after having unwittingly shattered his image, he withdraws, watching his reflection recompose itself. He realizes that a kiss is impossible. "One must not desire a reflection; a movement to possess it rends it. He is alone. What can he do? Contemplate."

Some critics have taken the proto-human Adam for the hero of the *Traité*, going so far, in some cases, as to see a heroic gesture in Adam's loss of Paradise. In the light of the essay, however, this position appears untenable, since Adam's gesture is tantamount to Narcissus' effort to possess his own reflection. Both lose all in the process, if only for a moment in the case of Narcissus. Both gestures are subject to censure on the grounds that they are acts of self-preference. One may argue that both acts are themselves manifestations of truths and, as such, required by the very ethics of Gide's theory. Gide's ethics, we recall, come into effect precisely because of the creation of time and apply to those caught in its flow. But, in Adam as well as in Narcissus, Gide was dealing directly with the Idea, with truths of Paradise; as such both antedate time and are not subject to the ethical principles that Gide sees as guides for all things in the temporal flow. Moreover, because both are Ideas, their gestures could not have been different.

The Poet is, like Narcissus and Adam, a perfect archetype. He rejects Adam's self-preference and incorporates Narcissus' activity. Although he is not the major figure of the *Traité*, it is his prime attribute that the whole essay develops. Like Gide's Narcissus, he has learned to contemplate, not his own reflection, but the reflection of reality in himself. However, he goes further and creates permanent and crystalline symbols of the truths he has perceived.

The Poet is a member of a chosen people; devoted to the perception and expression of the Idea he renounces self-exaltation in favor of what he has been chosen to represent. Thus Gide excuses himself in the epilogue for having repeated, perhaps even profaned, obvious truths; but the artist is driven to this because "he suffers if he admires alone, and would like others to adore as well."[37] Unlike Narcissus, who admires alone, the Poet and, of course, Gide, "represent."

As though in keeping with a self-imposed program of analysis, Gide limited himself in *Le Traité* to the problem of perception rather than that of expression. Its subtitle, *Théorie du symbole*, applies solely to a theory of reality.[38] He discusses the work of art and the expressive symbol in a single sentence. The work of art, he says, is a crystal in which the Idea flourishes in its purity, "où les phrases rythmiques et sûres, symboles encore, mais symboles purs, où les paroles, se font transparentes et révélatrices."[39] For the first time in the *Traité*, Gide here uses the word "symbole" to signify an expressive artistic unit. Throughout the work this term means the earthly representation of Idea. But only in this discussion of the work of art does he qualify this term with the emphatic phrase, "mais symboles purs," thus implying the fact that perception and not expression is his prime concern in the rest of the essay.

Gide's attitude towards the symbol as an expressive unit remains basically the same as in *Les Cahiers*. In both works the symbol accomplishes what discursive language cannot achieve, the synthetic representation of perceptual material. What differs is its subject matter. No longer at the service of the poet's emotion, the symbol becomes the form only he can give to an Idea perceived in reality. Instead of being exemplary he becomes a visionary in whom absolute truth lies latent.

In a letter to Paul Valéry written at the time Gide was writing *Le Traité* there is a passage that clarifies some of its notions.

Le livre n'est pas *nécessaire*. Et pourquoi faut-il qu'il y ait des livres? . . . Le hiéroglyphe *suffit* à murmurer les secrets de toute une science. . . . Mais on se prostitue pourtant parce qu'on a trop aimé les autres, faibles, et que par amour pour eux on *explique*.[40]

The Symbol: Practice and Theory

The paragraphs that introduce and terminate *Le Traité* say the very same thing. Like a refrain its last words take up again the theme of the usefulness of books but add an apology for the work itself. Unlike the priest, who wants to explain in order to be worshipped, the poet acts out of "an undying sympathy which has him unveil and profane, by revealing them, the most secret treasures of the temple." Here Gide makes explicit the poet's role as visionary.

Le Traité represents a denial of André Walter's most cherished aspiration. For although Walter insisted upon the maxim "il faut manifester" with equal ardor, his manifestations were pious exaltations of purity. In *Le Traité* Walter's poetry is completely absent; so too is his underlying belief in a universal moral standard of behavior. This standard and his sincere but vain attempt to abide by it formed the basis of his intimate drama. In *Le Traité*, however, Gide denies all moral norms other than the faithful representation of one's individual truth.

The contact with Mallarmé and the Symbolists, as Germaine Brée points out,[41] purified Gide of his romantic tendencies. In this contact too originated both Gide's infinite respect for the French language and the discovery of his own lyrical potential. To Mallarmé, Gide owes the conviction that the supremacy of art lies in its formal beauty, that he himself, incapable of lyrical outbursts, was nevertheless able to attain beauty in conceptual or intellectual terms, through the proper use of his own language.

What we learn from *Le Traité* is that the artist must contemplate himself with dispassion, disinterestedly; he must scrutinize external phenomena in the same manner, ascertaining the relationships between them and himself. While each thing that appears is an imperfect symbol, the poet too fabricates symbols, but of a different order, so that he may transmit to others his perceptions of Paradise.

Marcel Drouin immediately perceived the special achievements of *Le Traité*. In a letter to Gide he says:

> An extraordinary striving towards objectivity embellishes the myth. It has developed by itself, through your self-sacrifice; these are the blows which will kill Walter, if you still want to.[42]

Self-sacrifice for greater objectivity demonstrates the aesthetic efficacy of the essay's ideal.

What remained for Gide to do, after formulating the program of the *Traité*, was to follow it.

III

Le Voyage d'Urien:
Gide's Pathetic Fallacy

With *Le Traité du Narcisse*, Gide joined the Symbolists as a theoretician of the movement. *Le Voyage d'Urien*, written at irregular intervals during the last half of 1892 and published in January, 1893, satisfied, at least temporarily, his ambition to make for himself a place in the movement, not only as theoretician, but also as practicing artist. *Le Voyage d'Urien* is indeed a Symbolist novel about a typically Symbolist subject: reality mirrored in the poet's soul. The vehicle he chose was an imaginary voyage, an allegorical representation of a man's life.

The novel is divided into three parts plus a prelude and an envoi. Each part revolves about a major image that synthesizes each of the three modes of behavior considered by Gide to summarize man's alternatives. Since his imaginary voyage is an ocean trip, the three central images are seascapes. The first, "l'océan pathétique," reveals the temptations of sensuality. The adjective "pathétique" has here a strong connotation of physical feeling akin to the original Greek root *pathein*, meaning "to suffer physically." [1] The mariners of the *Orion* sail through a tropical sea; they make numerous stops to bathe in pastel-colored lagoons and to visit islands with lush growth, emitting heavy scents and decorated with "miraginous" cities and seductive sirens. The last and most conclusive sojourn is at the island realm of Queen Haiatalnefous. All but twelve of the travellers succumb to the charms of this feminine world and ultimately to the plague that destroys the flesh they so cherished. The stench of the decaying cadavers drives the abstainers away with the fate of the flesh clearly in mind.

Part Two, "La Mer des Sargasses," recounts the sluggish progress made by the *Orion* in still waters, dense with mud and seaweed. The central image synthesizes the feelings of inertia and boredom inherent in Gide's introspective alternative. The group of twelve dwindles to eight before the *Orion* breaks loose from the ensnaring seaweed and heads towards the cold waters of the Arctic.

In the "Voyage vers une mer glaciale," Part Three, they make their way towards "the divine city." They have prepared themselves for the absolute and ideal realms, Urien tells his comrades, by testing and proving the worth of their souls. By resisting the pleasures of the flesh and the lulling comforts of introspection, they have manifested their will. Now seven in number, the travellers abandon their ice-bound boat and proceed on foot to their goal, a calm, circular lake. Their quest at an end, the pilgrims no longer have a purpose; in a cold and apathetic state of will-lessness, they kneel on the shores of the lake seeking in its waters the realm of the Maker and wait to be absorbed by Him. "Et nous étant encore agenouillés, nous avons cherché sur l'eau noire le reflet du ciel que Je rêve." [2] The sudden use of the capitalized first-person-singular pronoun in a first-person-plural context suggests a unity or a common essence that Urien and his followers are about to reach. Because the pronoun is in the upper case, it acts like a proper noun, much like Rimbaud's famous "Je est un autre." [3] Though distinct from each member of the group, it comprehends them all. Into this "Je" coalesce the souls of the pilgrims, whether they be separate beings or merely extensions of Gide's own personality. In either case, the soul or souls wait to join their Maker at death. In the same manner that the lake reflects Heaven, the "Je" reflects it in its dreams. "Je" and the lake being thus identifiable with each other, they both represent the consciousness, and hence the presence, of God in the human being; both resemble outward manifestations of the Cartesian innate idea of God's existence.

Since Gide had never been to any of the places he describes, he peopled his voyage with images based upon books he had read and upon his own imagination.[4] These images, in addition to a richly rhythmical prose, make up the interest of the work.

Psychoanalytically-oriented critics have noticed that these images throw light upon Gide's homosexuality.[5] Gide had, at the time, only slight anxiety at most about his ultimate sexual preferences.[6] Yet, in *Le Voyage d'Urien*, he transcribed images whose full meaning he could not appreciate simply because he was being true to the ethics formulated in the Narcissus essay: he was manifesting. Although many of the feelings he dealt with were undelineated, "fluid," as he said in a later preface to the book,[7] he was acutely aware of their presence, if not of their roots. Also, however vague his feelings, the images he used were accurate translations of them; Gide's criteria were aesthetic, above all else.

A thorny problem arises from these considerations. How did Gide reconcile the ethic of the Narcissus essay with the apparent self-preference of *Le Voyage d'Urien*? The prime concern of the book appears to be, after all, Gide's own emotions, presented with more order and restraint than in *Les Cahiers*. Much later, in August, 1910, Gide said:

With the sole exception of *Le Voyage d'Urien*, I have never written a book without a deep need to write it; still,

Le Voyage d'Urien

I feel I have put much of myself in it and, for those who know how to read, this book, too, is revealing.[8]

These naive remarks would seem to indicate Gide's fidelity, at least in intent, to the Narcissus ethic for its deep-rooted motivations. The book was, admittedly, not concerned with the expression of his own personal drama and feelings. Yet, Gide affirms in the later preface, all the images in it were intended to communicate emotion, and the development of its plot suggests many of the same elements as Walter's intimate drama. Can it thus be assumed that Gide was following the aesthetic implicit in Le Traité by reflecting reality in the expression of emotions prompted by it? A clarification of the role the poet's emotion plays in the aesthetic process suggested by Le Traité will indicate how far Gide succeeded in following his own precepts.

Emotions, even though prompted by reality, are by definition subjective. Is not preoccupation with them self-preference, and does not self-preference itself require manifestation? Gide would say no to the first question; as for the second, he adds parenthetically to the last footnote of Le Traité: "By elevating oneself a bit, one sees, however, that everything manifests, but this should be recognized only afterwards." [9] That is, one ought not deliberately to give expression to the idea of self-preference. Like the person who refuses to manifest an idea, the egoist manifests by default, and thus both unconsciously represent the idea of error. For the artist in particular, however, the moral question revolves about the effective expression of his Idea, regardless of its own inherent moral value. For him, self-preference negates precisely his function. Through self-preference he tends to obstruct his perception of an idea or, at best, to subordinate the idea to its means of expression; that is, he chooses expressions according to criteria other than those the idea demands. Thus the

66

"immorality" of self-preference for the artist is of a special sort.

Now, with a clearer notion of the sin of self-preference, we can attempt an answer to our first question, is the artist's concern with his own emotions an expression of self-preference? Gide thinks not, and in *Le Traité du Narcisse*, by likening the Poet to Narcissus, he provides us with a rationale for artistic introspection. The goal of the poet is, after all, not the exaltation of his own emotions for themselves but their *mise en valeur* in a larger human context; they are, moreover, intimately connected with, if not the very substance of, his perception of the Absolute.

Lying dormant in the cosmos, *Le Traité du Narcisse* states, is Paradise, the garden of Ideas. All things created by Adam's fall come along in the river of time and little by little reveal to astute observers bits of Paradise. The sage and the seer perceive and collect these liberated bits in the Book of Wisdom. Now for Gide the archetypes of human emotions, too, float and circulate in the atmosphere, taking on different garbs at different places and periods of history. An emotion is not born, it simply *is*, he affirms in the preface to *Le Voyage d'Urien*:

> elle est depuis aussi longtemps que toutes choses qui la manifestent. Sa vie mystique à elle se passe à être *consentie* par les hommes . . . sa vie . . . est le besoin même de se manifester.[10]

Like any other phenomenon, because it issues from God, an emotion is thus indicative of some human truth, some idea with regard to man. If the total idea of man includes a description of his characteristics, these, in turn, are defined by the way he acts in and reacts to his natural habitat. Gide thought at this time that it was primarily through his emotions that man reacts to the world. Thus the artist who scrutinizes himself and his emotions does not commit the sin of self-preference so long as he uses his personal experience of emotion as a means to know and perceive its archetype. He must consider his own experience of emotion as a means whereby an archetypal emotion manifests itself and not as an end in itself.

Yet in *Le Voyage d'Urien*, there is evidence of some hesitation in abdicating self-preference. Gide's images, though inevitably tied to his own psychological bias, reveal his attempt at objective manifestation. He hoped, perhaps naively, to achieve at least a semblance of objectivity by expressing in a series of major images the emotions he felt latent in three alternative guides for men's behavior: sensuality; introspection; and idealism, with its inherent connotation of purity. Of course, these three alternatives closely reflect Gide's own personal preoccupations, the first and third being the basis for the intimate drama and the second, the mood of *Les Cahiers*. Gide admits, in the 1894 preface, that *Le Voyage* contains a personal vision of reality. The book's central emotion, he says, "is the very one evoked in us by the dream of life." But he goes further in the same paragraph: "my characterless sailors in turn become all of humanity, or are reduced to me alone." Thus a tension is born between subjectivity and objectivity, one that is further aggravated by the useless envoi. Here the author makes explicit what is implicit in the book's title and its suggestive pun, that the trip was nothing ("le voyage du rien"), no more than a dream elaborated in the quiet monotony of his study. This tension is responsible, too, for the underlying irony of the book, for only at the end, in the envoi, do we discover that the author, who urged action and travel, is himself victim of the inertia his travels were to cure. Thus there is an ambivalence of intention in *Le Voyage*: an urge to manifest emotion caused by reality on the one hand, and on the other, the inevitable return to himself and his own private dilemma.

In this book, Gide is primarily concerned with rendering as accurately as possible archetypes of the emotions aroused in him by several stages and attitudes of life. In order to create crystalline symbols of these archetypes he chose imagery as his medium. In *Les Cahiers*, we have seen, he also relied upon images to convey emotion. But there he felt no need to discover archetypes since, by his own definition, he was already archetypal; thus, however intimate, his emotions were indicative of the absolute, and the symbolic images constructed were made subservient to them. To attain the universal, he subsequently felt that he had to sacrifice the purely personal aspects of his feelings, and he sought the symbol of the archetype reflected in himself rather than the symbol of its reflection. In this way the symbolic images dictated by his own emotion would become, he felt, the archetypal emotion itself; the two fused in his mind. In the 1894 preface, he called these images landscapes.

Il me semble encore juste qu'une émotion que donne un paysage puisse se resservir de lui—*comme d'un mot*—et s'y reverser tout entière, puisqu'elle en fut à l'origine enveloppée. Emotion, paysage ne seront plus dès lors liés par rapport de cause à effet, mais bien par cette connexion indéfinissable, où plus de créancier et plus de débiteur,—par cette association du mot et de l'idée; du corps et de l'âme; de Dieu et de toute apparence.[11]

The fusion of the two elements in question (emotion and landscape or image) is so complete, the fluid emotion so takes the form of its landscape-image container, that one is indistinguishable from the other, that one indeed is the other.

Il y a là une sorte d'algèbre esthétique; émotion et manifeste forment équation; l'un est l'équivalent de l'autre. Qui dit *émotion* dira donc *paysage*; et qui lira *paysage* devra donc connaître *émotion*.[12]

The equivalence of emotion and landscape is not at all a new idea. It was in vogue at least by the time of the Romantics. But it was John Ruskin who, in his insistence upon truth in art, censured this equation and named it the "pathetic fallacy."[13] Schopenhauer, who, on the other hand, approved of the practice, quoted these lines of Byron:

> I live not in myself, but I become
> Portion of that around me; and to me
> High mountains are a feeling.[14]

In all probability Gide had this notion long before his contact with Schopenhauer, at least by his fifteenth or sixteenth year, when he began reading Amiel; for in the *Journal intime*, Amiel discusses and illustrates the equation "émotion-paysage":

> tous ces innombrables et merveilleux symboles que les formes, les couleurs, les végétaux, les êtres vivants, la terre et le ciel fournissent à toute heure à l'oeil qui sait les voir, m'apparaissaient charmants et saisissants. Je tenais la baguette poétique et n'avais qu'à toucher un phénomène pour qu'il me racontât sa signification morale. Un paysage quelconque est un état de l'âme, et qui lit dans tous deux est émerveillé de retrouver la similitude dans chaque détail.[15]

Similar notions can be found in Gide's earliest writings; in the *Notes d'un voyage en Bretagne* made during the summer of 1889, he stated:

Le Voyage d'Urien

Il me semblait que le paysage n'était plus qu'une émanation de moi-même projetée . . . il dormait avant ma venue, inerte et virtuel, et je le créais pas à pas en percevant ses harmonies; j'en étais la concience même.[16]

These landscapes, then, became the symbols of emotions he felt obliged to manifest. In short, they represent a highly specialized yet universal vocabulary.

Although Gide wrote the 1894 preface after the publication of *Le Voyage d'Urien*, there is evidence that the ideas here formulated were not arrived at a posteriori; while in a philosophical frame of mind, he returned to these ideas, after brief treatment in his earlier years, and clarified them before and during the composition of *Le Voyage*. In an effort to correct the bad influence of Oscar Wilde, he plunged into technical and philosophical literature. "With him," Gide said of Wilde, "I had forgotten how to think," and in order to relearn the art of thinking, he began studying the problem of language in addition to reading several technical and scientific books.[17]

In *De l'Origine du langage*, which Gide was reading at this time, Ernest Renan discusses the double aspect of language. On the one hand, he says, the grammar of a language is a product of the intelligence, of pure reason, whereas the matter and substance itself of language, its words, depend upon sensation, or the sensitivity.

A study of the most ancient languages discloses this fact in a striking way. Whereas their grammatical structure contains the deepest metaphysics, one can see in every word a material concept becoming the symbol of an idea. It appears that primitive man did not live at all within himself, but lived diffused in the world from which he barely distinguished himself.

71

As though for official support in a convincing argument, he quotes these lines from Maine de Biran: "Man does not begin by separating himself from the objects of his representation; he exists entirely outside of himself; nature is he, he is nature." "Thus," Renan continues, "*alienated from himself*, he becomes, as Leibniz says, the concentric mirror in which is reflected that nature of which he is a part." [18]

Thus, Gide found in Renan historic and linguistic corroboration of the theories so evident in *Le Voyage*. Moreover, the process at work in the development of ancient languages as described by Renan had particular appeal precisely because it was primeval and concerned the roots of man. The fusion of emotion and landscape was all the more valid for Gide's purposes because it appeared to be inherent in the nature of man and thus offered a way to approach the universal and the absolute.

In *Le Voyage d'Urien* the concept of the symbol seems to differ somewhat from that of *Le Traité*. Upon closer scrutiny one can see that this difference can be attributed to a change in point of view rather than to a change in attitude, for in essence this attitude remains the same. In *Le Traité* Gide considers the symbol from a transcendental point of view; that is, from a more than human vantage point. He sought the objectivity of God to render a view of the cosmos and to define the poet's role in obtaining knowledge of this cosmos. What is at issue is the perception of truths and not the process involved in their expression, which *Le Traité* merely illustrates obliquely. The task of the poet, he said, is precisely to recognize that what *is* is a forest of symbols and to perceive the absolutes these symbols both conceal and reveal. For this reason the central image, Narcissus, the beholder or contemplative nature, is also the aesthetic symbol of the perceptual effort of the poet. The problem in *Le Voyage*, as in *Les Cahiers*, is not the perception of truths but their accurate and artistic expression. Here, the initial process of perception, the subject of *Le Traité*, is supposedly done; what remains is the problem of recasting perception into crystalline symbols. It is important to understand that both books include two kinds of symbols, one natural, phenomenological, and imperfect, the other artificial, aesthetic, and crystalline. Narcissus, as beholder, is the aesthetic symbol of the perceptual powers, not the natural sign. But he is engaged in exploring the natural symbols that constitute the world.

The nature of the emotion expressed and its relationship to Gide differs, it was suggested earlier, in *Les Cahiers* and *Le Voyage*. In the first, complex emotions in their intensity and immediacy were all-important; images and symbols were sought to render them faithfully, and they varied while Gide's emotions persisted. In *Le Voyage*, however, once an emotion "chose" its image, he developed the image in detail, using his feelings only as guide. The object of his art was no longer the faithful reproduction of complex feelings but their elevation to a more general, human level. It was imperative, before this could begin, to isolate one facet of his emotions; so Gide renounced all others to be faithful to this isolated facet and its concretization. He developed and analyzed in each of the three major images of the book just one facet of his feelings. Synthesis, the aim of *Les Cahiers*, here yielded to analysis.

In *Le Voyage* Gide's different attitude towards his emotions is further reflected in the deliberate alienation of his principal character from himself. The relationship between the author and his protagonist has changed drastically. Urien is no longer a double of his creator. He is merely an example of "l'homme vraiment homme" seeking who he is. Unlike André Walter, he is not preoccupied with his emotions or with their aesthetic expression. His sole purpose is self-exploration; following the ethic of the Narcissus essay, he knows he must manifest his essence, and he therefore travels through the world seeking situations to precipitate revelatory actions.[19] Again unlike Walter, he is not mystical or on a constant search for the symbolic value of phenomena; in matters of symbols he is totally naive and accepts and reacts to all about him with candor. The landscapes he visits are real, and by reacting to them he defines himself. He resists the temptations of "la mer pathétique," remains free in the emprisoning marshes of the Sargasso, and bypasses the rigor of Eskimo theology. Only in the severity of his abstinence do we catch a refracted glimpse of his own emotions. But he is in no way self-conscious about them. He merely reacts and transcribes in his logbook what happens. Thus, practically emotionless and characterless, Urien and his companions are oblivious to the ultimate symbolic value of the landscapes they pass through.

This value is made apparent through the clash between figures and landscapes. Each of these two elements alone would have little significance. The pilgrims affirm their personalities and unconsciously give meaning to the scenery about them only by passing through and reacting to it. They are, thus, essential to the full comprehension of Gide's symbolic landscapes. And because they and their secretary are oblivious, Urien's factual account of their exploits is necessarily understated; this reinforces the evocative power of the book's symbols, for only in the mind of the reader does the full significance of the clash between figures and landscapes materialize.

It is nevertheless with the landscape images that Gide was primarily and originally concerned. Several of the minor images of *Le Voyage*, as well as two major ones he expanded into landscapes, had already been present in a series of poems Gide wrote during 1891 and attributed to André Walter.[20] Two images can be traced to *Les Cahiers* themselves. The image of the reading lamp, which Walter evolved in the notebooks as a symbol of sympathetic study and introspection, occurs again in *Les Poésies*. But here it no longer has the soul-stirring force it had for him in *Les Cahiers*; now it is rather a symbol of inactivity, of vain discussions, to be abandoned in favor of involvement in life. In *Les Poésies*, Walter and his "amie" remain inactive despite themselves but seek to abandon the limited world their reading lamp circumscribes.

Une lampe neuve remplace la vide;
Une nuit succède à une autre nuit;
Et l'on entend fuir dans la nuit le bruit
Du sablier triste qui se vide.
Nous rapetassons de faux syllogismes
Et nous ergotons sur la Trinité,
Mais tout ça, ça manque un peu de lyrisme
Et nos lampes ne font pas beaucoup de clarté.[21]

The limited world of Walter's lamp yields to the wide world of the archetypal lamp, the sun, in *Le Voyage d'Urien*. This banal comparison, though not stated, is implicit in the opening lines of Urien's logbook. "Sans que je m'en fusse aperçu, ma lampe s'était éteinte; devant l'aube s'était ouverte ma croisée." [22]

The snow image, perhaps the more important one taken from *Les Cahiers*, undergoes several transformations in *Les Poésies* and in *Le Voyage*. It represents Walter's ideals, purity and the absolute. But it also has a strong therapeutic power in *Les Cahiers*. Alone in his mountain retreat and subject to "the restlessness of a vagabond puberty," Walter subjects himself to long walks on the mountain in order to maintain control over his rebellious flesh. On the road he sees mountains, forests, barely visible snow caps, villages with strange names; "Bluffy," he adds finally, "the name of a fiord, cold, nordic, blue with mist . . . and then I left without seeing anything else, leaving behind something like a wake of tenderness." [23]
The meaning is clear: the central image, the fiord, comes to

signify not only purity but his achievement, however temporary, of this purity. At the end of the notebooks and near the height of his madness, the image of Bluffy comes back to haunt him.[24] Finally, desperately desiring the purity he is unable to attain, he runs out into the snow, where he dies. The last line of the notebooks synthesizes Walter's purity fixation: "the snow is pure." In the poems the snow image becomes "lustral water," which, after having "filtered down from the melancholy glacier,"[25] cures the sickly couple. So too, in *Le Voyage*, Morgain's mysterious fever, caused by bathing in too tepid pools, is cured by the magic of "the eternal snow." "Eau de glace," Urien thus begins his eulogy of the health-bringing water,

> qui pourra dire ta pureté! . . . Elle était si pure qu'elle grisait comme l'air très matinal des montagnes . . . elle a lavé la flétrissure des fièvres et sa délicate vertu a glissé jusqu'à nos pensées, comme d'une eau lustrale.[26]

The color blue, which recalls Mallarmé's "Azur," and the snow-capped mountains merge with the prime image of snow into the last landscape of *Le Voyage*, "la mer glaciale." Here in the cold, desolate landscapes, where life and warmth are barely maintained, the dangers of an exaggerated desire for purity, with a resulting abstinence from life's functions, become apparent. The eight remaining sailors fall victim to scurvy, and, unable to continue their voyage, they indolently remain on board the idle ship. All but one of the party are revived by the hemostatic liquid that Eric, the most vigorous of the group, had found. Eric had earlier broken the stark equilibrium of the Arctic realms by distinguishing life from mere existence. By wantonly destroying guillemot eggs and eiders he introduced death into the barren landscape, thus affirming life. He repeated this affirmation by stealing the lifesaving liquid from the Eskimos. These natives apparently used the liquid, but, unlike the sailors of the *Orion*, they remain fixed in their milieu, unaware of the complexity of life, of the Absolute, of their own existence. Revived, the sailors try to proceed to their goal; but the *Orion* becomes icebound. They abandon and burn their boat and enter at last into the realm of the Absolute, where time and movement cease.

The basic image of mud and still waters expanded into the second landscape, "la mer des Sargasses," appears previously only in *Les Poésies*. The poem "Polders" evokes a mood of indolence and monotony typical of the marshland it describes, but only in the last two poems of the collection does the inhibiting force of stagnant waters and mud prevent the lovers from attaining their ideal. Thus the symbol is first clarified here. In "Promontoire," whose promontory may be considered a horizontal mountain jutting out into the blue, the couple are eager to reach the sea but are detained by the mud.

> Nos pieds nus se sont enfoncés dans la vase.
> O tache sur la peau délicate!—un peu d'eau claire
> Où tremper ses pieds nus dans le flot de la mer.[27]

In the last poem, they cross a marshy plain; they wearily arrive at the doors of a large church but find they are too late to be admitted.

> Je crois que ce que nous aurions de mieux à faire
> Ce serait de tâcher de nous rendormir.[28]

These final lines close the collection and point out the sickness of "la mer des Sargasses."

The images and the landscape of the first part of *Le Voyage* are entirely new to Gide. Their sources, however, as Justin O'Brien points out, are predominantly literary: *The Arabian*

Nights, Rimbaud's "Bateau ivre," the *Odyssey,* and a curious insertion from *Die Lehrlinge zu Sais* of Novalis.[29] "Le Voyage sur l'océan pathétique" is a catalogue of sensual temptations affecting each of the five senses. As was his practice, Gide slowly prepared the full import of the final landscape from the very early days of the voyage. The pilgrims of the *Orion* are quickly chased from the first island they stop at by the heavy, intoxicating perfume emanating from the lush growth.

Les parfums étouffants qui montaient de toute l'île et que le vent rabattait vers nous, les parfums qui déjà nous troublaient de vertige, nous eussent, je crois, fait mourir. Ils étaient si denses qu'on en voyait la poussière aromale tournoyer.[30]

This last sensual metaphor introduces an atmosphere of close correspondence between the various sensory impressions pervading the entire first part of *Le Voyage.* "The softness of the calm and tepid waves filled us," [31] Urien observes. Soon after, on another island and with their languor reinforced by a nap on the warm beach, several of the mariners see a vision of a fantastic Near-Eastern city, "the color of dawn and Moslem." From the minarets come sounds of music "so wondrous that we were transfixed with ecstasy." [32] Drawn on by the enchanting sight and sound, they try to reach this city, but it vanishes before their eyes. What appears instead is a bevy of sirens that frighten the men back to the *Orion.* But two weeks later, several members of the group return from a foraging trip laden with strange fruit and smirking ironically. The virtuous members are frightened by the luster of the fruit and refuse to eat it; thus a rift develops between the two groups. The foragers sneer at the others and cynically recount to their horrified listeners their amorous exploits of the night ashore. "Keenly feeling what we did not want to be," Urien notes in his journal, "we began to know what we were." [33] Developing and fortifying their will to resist sensual enticement, the abstainers thus prepare for the supreme test, which is fully developed in the last island, the realm of Queen Haiatalnefous. Here all but twelve succumb to the joys of the flesh.

Gide, in this meditation on sensuality, thus uses visual, auditory, tactile, olfactory, and gustatory images, all interwoven into the rich fabric of a sensual landscape. The emotion this landscape develops is passion underlined by the ferocity of abstinence and resistance demonstrated by the virtuous twelve.

The theme of water, Delay rightly points out,[34] has symbolic value in Le Voyage. We have considered the therapeutic force contained in mountain water. This power is especially evident in the first part of the book. But here, cold, pure water is contrasted to the debilitating effects of the tepid waters of the tropics. As the virtuous mariners become more and more sensitive to the appeals of the flesh they also become more and more reluctant to bathe in the rose-colored sea. The events of their voyage are frequently punctuated, and as though commented upon, by Urien's "we bathed" or "we did not bathe on that day." The day of the encounter with the sirens, they do not bathe "for fear of them." But Morgain falls silent and Urien understands that "he longs for the sirens." [35] Morgain soon comes down with a mysterious fever that is finally cured by the purifying mountain water. Here the connection between the aphrodisiac water of "la mer pathétique" and the purifying mountain liquid is firmly established. These considerations bring to mind another possible source of the book's imagery, the Bible. In I Corinthians 10, Paul recalls several events of the early books of the Old Testament. "They drank of that spiritual Rock that followed them and that Rock was Christ . . . we should not lust after evil things, as they also lusted . . . neither let us commit fornication, as some of them committed and fell in one day three and twenty thousand." What destroyed the sinners of the Old Testament was a plague, to which Gide's fornicators also succumbed. Thus, although Gide's main concern was a sensual landscape connoting passion, the import of Part One is indeed the same virtue of resistance and abstinence urged by Paul.

Urien's imagery, though Gide's prime interest, was also his most vulnerable point. Speaking in particular of *Les Poésies d'André Walter*, Germaine Brée makes the following observations:

> Gide lacks one of the essential elements of poetry, the image. He succeeds in clothing his emotion with only a literary or conventional vocabulary.[36]

This judgment is applicable to *Le Voyage* as well; many of the images, the idea itself of a symbolic voyage, were literary commonplaces. Some transformed by his fancy are striking, but most were, no doubt unconsciously, taken from external sources in compensation for his incapacity to grasp external phenomena and to perceive latent and fresh correspondences between them and his own interior state. Paul Valéry, in an extremely perceptive critique of the book, observed that "the images are often a bit . . . gross; resonant, I might say"; they betray a preference for rendering an object at the expense of integrating it into the whole of the work.

> I repeat; you insist, I believe, too much upon your book and not enough upon yourself. You wanted to embellish it with everything that seemed beautiful—but beware of Literature (*idola libri*). The subtle relationships in a book . . . are terribly exact.

Again, sensing Gide's literary eclecticism, he observed cryptically, "a variety of scents: Flaubert, *passim*. Barrès, Maeterlinck." [37] Stephen Ullmann, on the other hand, finds that "the most striking feature of the imagery is its appropriateness: it is perfectly adapted to the tone of each of the three phases and contributes in no small measure to creating the distinctive atmosphere of each section." [38] Germaine Brée sees themes and images as consciously ordered: "they are learned aesthetic exercises, a bit artificial, but carefully controlled." [39] These opinions are tenable, but if we extend them further we find that the prime fault of the work, however artificial, is that the guideline for the images is not the landscape but the atmosphere and the emotion that first yielded it. Thus the images, though rigorously worked out and ordered, were done so only according to a standard existing outside of the work rather than falling into place through the logic inherent in the aesthetic organism itself. The fanciful details and images of Part One, for example, elaborate rather than develop the major image. At the end, on the island of Queen Haiatalnefous, we observe the intensity of emotion rather than experience a more profound understanding of it. Moreover, the intensity of emotion results from the accumulation in one place and time of all the disparate sensual enticements scattered throughout the earlier part of the book.

Thus Gide was still unable to cut his emotional ties to his work despite all his efforts to the contrary. He was still too close to the feelings he hoped to immortalize in art.

IV

Two Images: The Egg of the Cuttlefish and the Swamp

In his *Oeuvres complètes*, Gide's fourth prose work *La Tentative amoureuse* follows immediately upon *Le Traité du Narcisse*. This is clearly an error if the editor, Louis Martin-Chauffier, and Gide himself, who closely supervised the edition, intended to respect chronological order. For *La Tentative* was written after *Le Voyage d'Urien* and before his departure for North Africa in October, 1893.[1] But this error is even further compounded. The prologue of *La Tentative* was placed on the same page as the epilogue of *Le Traité*, thus becoming incorporated into the Narcissus essay. The definitive text of *La Tentative*, which has appeared unmutilated in other editions, was again established by Jean-Jacques Thierry in the Pléiade edition of Gide's *Romans, récits et soties, oeuvres lyriques*.

The important preface to the work was fortunately not misplaced in the *Oeuvres complètes*. In it Gide suggests a theory of the artist's relationship to his work that applies to most of his own fiction.

Nos livres n'auront pas été les récits très véridiques de nous-mêmes,—mais plutôt nos plaintifs désirs, le souhait d'autres vies à jamais défendues, de tous les gestes impossibles . . . chaque livre n'est plus qu'une tentation différée.[2]

Unable to satisfy his vague desire for action in and commitment to a real world, Gide, unconsciously at first, turned to his art. Writing *Les Cahiers* and *Le Voyage* temporarily satisfied his needs, but not until he began *La Tentative* did he become conscious of the value fiction offers as a form of experience. In a frequently quoted journal entry dated 1893 Gide carefully analyzed the effect that the creation of a work of art has upon its author.

Le sujet agissant c'est soi; la chose rétroagissante, c'est un sujet qu'on imagine. C'est donc une méthode d'action sur soi-même, indirecte, que j'ai donné là; et c'est aussi tout simplement un conte.[3]

These considerations led to the ideas expounded in the preface. "Literature, then, can become a substitute for experience —for him who writes it," Justin O'Brien concludes in his discussion of the work. "The Foreword to the *Tentative* is a capital document because it offers the first statement of this theory of personal catharsis which was to find such frequent restatement throughout Gide's work." [4]

La Tentative amoureuse is closely allied to its predecessor, *Le Voyage d'Urien*. But instead of reflecting states of mind through an imaginary voyage in space, *La Tentative* achieves the same end by an imaginary voyage in time. "I wanted to describe a relationship between the seasons and the soul," [5] the narrator says. But since its subtitle is *Le Traité du vain désir*, more emphasis is placed on Urien's "mer pathétique," that is, on questions of the flesh and of desire. Luc and Rachel are young lovers who, after some hesitation, consummate their love. Spring passes to summer and hesitation to full experience of joy. But autumn brings the monotony of repeated happiness, and finally the lovers part, unable to transcend themselves and their all-inclusive passion. Luc thus learns, after the fact, the virtue of Urien's tenaciously practiced abstinence; he comes to acknowledge that passion is ephemeral by nature and that it fixes our whole being upon ephemera, eventually turning everything into ashes.[6] Passion, Gide affirms in the conclusion, as an expression of self-preference, detains us from our goal, which is God, the eternal that ever lies before us, or the full realization of all our potentials.

Through Luc and Rachel, Gide's attempt at love was ideally consummated. By isolating a tendency perceived within himself and permitting it to develop in his imagination, he experimented with a mode of behavior but avoided its unhappy consequences. He later described this process even more fully.

> Que de bourgeons nous portons en nous . . . qui n'écloront jamais que dans nos livres! . . . Pour créer un héros ma recette est bien simple: Prendre un de ces bourgeons, le mettre en pot—tout seul—on arrive bientôt à un individu admirable.[7]

His treatment of the image remains, with one important exception, the same as in *Le Voyage d'Urien*. Seasons instead of landscapes synthesize the lovers' different emotions. An impenetrable walled garden, like the closed church in *Les Poésies d'André Walter*, and the walled-in lake open only to the assiduous Urien and his companions, suggest the goal Luc and Rachel lose sight of. Also, the sea, which drew Urien on, slowly awakens in Luc an awareness of his sacrifice and of all that awaits him elsewhere, thus suggesting the theme of departure similarly expressed in *Les Poésies* and *Le Voyage*. One new image, however, among all the familiar ones in *La Tentative*, strikes the reader's attention: the cuttlefish egg. Its

Two Images

strangeness is emphasized by the contrast it makes with the book's more conventional images and the feelings they represent.

These feelings, developed earlier in *Le Voyage* in the form of the first landscape and echoing the Pauline admonition against fornication, form the substance of the whole *Traité du vain désir*. Like Gide's first essay, *Le Traité du Narcisse*, the present one is a demonstration, but it demonstrates a principle more intimate than its predecessor: the vanity and waste of desire. This principle is obviously a rationalization of Gide's deep-rooted and ambivalent impulses: a desperate attraction to, and a morbid fear of, conventional carnal love. Thus the initial image in *La Tentative amoureuse*, of a group of barefooted girls emerging from the woods at dawn, "wild and wet from the grass, their hair still undone from the night before," [8] evokes a suppressed excitement in Luc analogous to the sensual frenzy of "La Mer pathétique" and "Le Cahier noir." But since Gide's thesis is that desire is vain, he is bent upon showing that when satisfied it burns itself out, leaving nothing behind. Thus when Luc's desire is allayed and he lapses, along with his partner, into the monotony of relentless happiness, boredom and sterility become the dominant moods. What results resembles the state of mind brought on by a sterile relationship. A similarly neutral "état d'âme" pervades the second part of *Le Voyage d'Urien*, it is true; but it is especially evident, in terms of a human couple, in *Les Poésies*. In this latter case boredom is due not to carnal intimacy but rather to abstinence. Yet the feelings are the same and the images used to convey them are similar. Boredom then follows satisfied passion in *Le Traité du vain désir* as it does repressed passion in *Les Poésies*.[9]

It is in this imagistic and emotional context that the cuttlefish image appears. Luc and Rachel have been walking on the beach.

En revenant, Rachel trouva, sur le sable, un oeuf de sèche, énorme, noir, élastique, et d'une bizarrerie de forme comme intentionnelle, tellement qu'ils la jugèrent importante pour eux.[10]

This image introduces into a rather regular and uneventful situation at least a note of irregularity and perhaps a note of exoticism and mystery. Because of its extraordinary and bizarre qualities it clashes with the central images of the book, by its very presence inviting consideration of what lies beyond the emotional and experiential continuum delineated by Luc and Rachel. Its function, then, is to jar, and it succeeds in dislodging both Luc and Rachel, if not the reader as well, from intense passion become monotonous.

The image of the cuttlefish egg represents a phenomenological entity and is one that lay beyond Gide's usual imagistic banalities. Once committed to paper it came to exist independently of his emotions, and was born and is justifiable in terms of the work alone. The cuttlefish egg acts as the object itself, presenting its own virtues; it does not appear, as do most previous Gidian images, only because of the qualities it shares with something less palpable and more abstract. Unlike the landscapes of *Le Voyage* and *La Tentative*, which are reflections of emotions designed to evoke them, the cuttlefish egg does not reflect but only evokes. Like the broken piano string of *Les Cahiers*, it is a pure expressive symbol; unlike its predecessor, however, it functions alone on the level of the characters and not simultaneously as a reflection of Gide's own real feelings.

The bizarre quality of the cuttlefish egg points to the image's function. Its unusual nature suggests mystery and exoticism; because it comes from the sea it points to the wonders the sea can offer. "And suddenly Rachel felt uneasy: she sensed that Luc was beginning to think." Watching him contemplate the sea, she quickly perceives "an anguish and thirst for adventure." [11] A moment later their attention is attracted by the sun's reflection on the forbidding gates of an unknown park. It is at this moment, after these common Gidian images, that Rachel finds the egg. The last image thus comprehends at once the two previous ones, as well as synthesizes the point of the story. For the egg reveals the existence of something beyond them, an experience their all-encompassing love keeps them from knowing.

The importance of this symbolic image in Gide's aesthetic development lies in its opening the path his subsequent symbols and images will follow. It points to the independence his symbols are to obtain from the rigid control of the thing symbolized; they will have a life of their own, evolve and assume character traits or tones independently of their tenor. They will no longer merely represent but suggest and evoke. Thus Gide began as early as *La Tentative* to move away from sole concern with the tenor towards a fuller development of the vehicle, attributing to it the major value and seeking in it the possible source of new and undiscovered truths.

The aesthetic efficacy of these ideas is fully revealed in Gide's next published work, *Paludes*. As has so often been mentioned, *Paludes* is a parody of Gide's Symbolist period. A breath of fresh air in the "serres chaudes" of Symbolism, the book prepared the way for the explosion of *Les Nourritures terrestres*. The techniques Gide favored earlier are parodied and ridiculed by *reductio ad absurdum*. The title itself suggests the state of mind evoked in the book; so, too, does the title of another book to be written by the protagonist, *Polders*. The formula "paysage = état d'âme" appears over and over again in the form of bogs, fens, and hot-houses. Through all this faintly appears the smile of the bemused Gide, indulging and mocking his youthful fancies. The book has its serious moments, to be sure, but even these are in a party atmosphere. "I'm working on *Paludes*," he wrote to a friend in May, 1894:

> I hope to make people laugh and think; you'll see that I have put myself in it. Besides, it is a satire of ourselves.[12]

Germaine Brée is perfectly right in observing that *Paludes* takes as its point of departure the point of arrival of the earlier works.[13] In *Le Traité du Narcisse, Le Voyage d'Urien,* and *La Tentative amoureuse,* Gide was intent upon creating a central image and developing within it all that was wholly commensurate with his emotional state of mind. Seeking the landscape appropriate to his frame of mind, he was primarily concerned with the proper construction of this symbol. In *Paludes,* however, the central image has already been obtained; the task of reducing an emotion to its simplest and purest pictorial equivalent has been done long before the book's action even begins. Thus freed from external influences or justifications which would require continual reference to Gide's own emotions, the image enjoys unlimited associative privileges in his fictional world. Because of this purity and intensity the image can color or attract to itself all that has even the slightest trait in common with it. The dominant image of *Paludes,* which gives the book its title, remains safely tucked away in a typically Gidian container, the work within a work.

The narrator of Gide's book is never described but is occasionally explained and frequently illustrated. Like so many of Gide's writings, *Paludes* is in the form of a journal; it is kept for a period of six days by a man of letters who does not identify himself and who is in the throes of composing a book inspired by a glance at his own life. His feeling of utter monotony, compounded with the idea of a victim of this monotony who proves at first powerless and then, by force of habit and human adaptability, reluctant to break the stagnant mood of his life, suggests to our unnamed narrator the Virgilian figure of Tityrus in his first eclogue. He makes Tityre, *semper recubans*, forever reclining, the protagonist of his own story. Tityre does nothing, or very little, but pass time, whereas our narrator is busy writing *Paludes*. He is also involved in several personal relationships (Hubert, Richard, Angèle) and takes prominent part in the literary activities and functions about him. But it is precisely the monotonous regularity of his life, which for some reason he suddenly becomes aware of, that gives him the feelings responsible for his book. This fact, however, is fully revealed to us only later, at a point in the book where the swamp image has colored both his own and the reader's way of looking at his activities. At first he tells us that Tityre is Richard, the poor and wretched hack who is convinced he is leading a full and active life. Finally, owing to his insistence, we begin to view his own activities as humdrum, his attempts at action as feeble, his own situation as paludal. Unlike Tityre and Richard, he sees Parisian life, literary activity, and his own involvement in both as paludal; but he also makes an attempt to do something about it. He tries, for example, to pry loose all his friends and acquaintances and especially himself. But he does not succeed in breaking out of his own marshland, and becomes Tityre. Like his hero he fails because he cannot venture forth into the unknown; the stagnant atmosphere of his life, however dull, is nevertheless safely familiar.

At the end of Gide's story, the narrator undertakes a new work entitled *Polders*. His decision to compose a variant of his initial subject recalls the earlier pose of Tityre fishing. Tityre is unsuccessful, and to increase his chances he increases the number of his lines. But to no avail; he cannot catch a thing. He increases his lines; the writer tries another call to action. Of necessity neither can break out of his mold. The nature of this necessity is elicited by Angèle when she asks why Tityre cannot catch any fish. The narrator answers that it is primarily aesthetic, dictated by "la vérité du symbole," by the requirements of symbolic truth. If he were to succeed, he would be a different symbol of a different truth.

> J'arrange les faits de façon à les rendre plus conformes à la vérité que dans la réalité . . . les événements sont appropriés aux caractères; c'est ce qui fait les bons romans; rien de ce qui nous arrive n'est fait pour autrui. Hubert aurait déjà fait là une pêche miraculeuse! Tityre ne prend rien: c'est d'une vérité psychologique.[14]

Despite the levity of tone and homeliness of illustration, the observations made to satisfy Angèle's curiosity are extremely pertinent to the aesthetic principles in operation in Gide's own work. Gide is not interested in making his work conform to reality but rather to a higher, aesthetic reality as exemplified in the work of art. "La vérité du symbole" means consistency, hence intensity, of the symbolic image, which is shorn of all that would dilute it were it to reflect the inconsistencies and irrelevancies of real life. Because he proposes to arrange facts according to a truth, or even to an idea, his work is inevitably artificial; contained in a given image, it is subject only to the dictates of reason in its execution and development. Gide came to see that a work of art is precisely "a work of reason," that its virtue is artificiality.[15] The artist, he felt, condenses experience into pure artistic form devoid of the real world's diffusion and diversity. "L'oeuvre d'art," Gide said five years later, "est une oeuvre de distillation; l'artiste est un bouilleur de cru. Pour une goutte de ce fin alcool, il faut une somme énorme de vie, qui s'y concentre."[16] The swamp image of *Paludes* and Tityre himself are such distillations. Carried through Gide's *Paludes* in his narrator's work, the image sheds its light upon all it approaches. And the one closest to the source is, of course, his unnamed protagonist.

Richard, the narrator frequently suggests, is his contemporary model for Tityre, and Hubert provokes a justification of the book, but it is his literary angel, Angèle, that stimulates the longest discussion of his novel, because she is the most patient and apparently the most interested. It is only to Angèle that he exposes the mechanics of *Paludes*. He explains to her his use of the symbol and its relationship to reality, or more accurately, to the emotions reality stimulated in him. In a later discussion he further clarifies this relationship. Admitting that Richard is Tityre, he states that although Richard is married and has a family, he has imagined Tityre alone; he has condensed this family, with their variety of interests and activities, into a single literary entity in order to concentrate the monotony of their lives. He thereby subordinates respect for fact to intensity of expression. "The important thing is that I convey the emotion they evoke in me." [17] But earlier he admitted that the subject matter of his book is precisely the emotion a view of his own life evokes in him. These affirmations are not mutually exclusive if we consider that he sees in Richard an exaggeration of what he senses in himself and thus is himself especially sensitive to Richard's behavior. In the final analysis, then, it is his own emotion and his own life that he is essentially concerned with and that he distills in the swamp image in a roundabout effort to alter his own condition.

The writer not only recounts *Paludes* to Angèle, he lives it in her company. It is with her that he plans and executes his great journey, which amounts finally to a mere stroll in a suburban park. He is greatly disturbed by the failure of his "tiny trip" to effect a liberation from the monotony of his existence. The following day he admits: "It seems to me that I am still carrying *Paludes* with me." [18]

Although the narrator discusses different aspects of his book with different people, there is one cardinal point he does not explain. His prime interest, "the emotions [his] life gave [him] . . . boredom, futility, monotony," [19] is supposedly epitomized by the swamp image. Yet in his discussions he always talks only about Tityre, the human figure in this landscape. On the other hand, in those parts of his book reproduced in his journal he emphasizes the landscape itself. The relationship between the two reveals still another dimension in Gide's concept of the image.

In painting, a landscape may be considered the projection of a human feeling; it necessarily presupposes a human being observing it and reacting in the person both of the artist who was moved to paint it and the spectator for whom it was executed. But a human figure may even be painted into the scene as a sample of the artist's intended audience. An observer himself, this figure remains apart from the landscape, yet, by his very presence there, suggests that it is to be observed and that its model, in reality, can be seen by human eyes. Moreover, he can demonstrate how the artist intended his landscape to be viewed; by reacting to it accordingly, with an expression or posture of awe, fear, nostalgia, he characterizes the emotions the artist hopes to evoke. But if the figure is active and functions in the world of the scene depicted he becomes a part of it and is oblivious of the meaning it has for the artist and spectator alike. In either case he adds a human dimension to the scene. Thus whenever a figure appears in a landscape painting he inevitably augments its tension, for he establishes a human foothold in nature and suggests that the world is man's sphere of activity, his home. Tityre in the swamp serves this function; through his involvement in and reaction to the central image he compounds in purely human terms the stagnancy inherent in the swamp.

But *Paludes* is more than a landscape with a human figure in it. A painting can have its own rhythm and movement, but it is always within a domain fixed by immediate perception. Human time, the perception of change and its significance, is nonexistent in painting, whereas it is the most essential element of narration. Thus Tityre can relate to the swamp (and, by extension, the narrator can relate to his society) in a way the figure in a painting cannot. For although a mood may be conveyed in fiction by a landscape the human figure passing through and interrelating with it introduces the dynamics of reciprocal influence. Tityre admires the view from his window, he goes fishing and hunting, takes long walks through the landscape that reveal wonders ordinarily imperceptible to the non-paludal-oriented eye. He finally buys an aquarium in order to have a replica of the swamp in his own house. In this manner the swamp image grows as he becomes more and more absorbed by it. He adds to the static landscape an element of movement, development, reaction, and struggle. Gide exploited these possibilities and thus greatly enlarged the facets of his landscape-emotion symbol. Tityre fusing with the swamp image is richer by far than the swamp image alone, richer indeed than Urien, Luc, and Rachel, who function principally as observers and suggest their creator's feelings about what they see.

If for the narrator of *Paludes*, and Gide too, the marshland represents the distillate of a human emotion, *ennui*, then the human who makes his own this stagnant landscape is another distillate, of something else. For he must indeed be a rare creature to survive in so rarefied an atmosphere. But although sloth, acceptance, sterility, and ineffectuality are the sole elements of Tityre's personality, he still represents a human being, with whom the reader must identify himself. Through their common humanness Tityre exerts a sway over the reader, forcing him to accept that aspect of himself of which Tityre is the pure essence. Tityre's personality is not dependent upon the swamp image, of course. But it complements the swamp and gives it human significance.

In talking about *Paludes* the narrator describes it differently to everyone. In the longest chapter of the book, and at Angèle's banquet, someone points out this inconsistency. Undaunted, he answers that "the only way to recount the same thing to each one is to change the form to suit each new spirit." But he does finally attempt to explain what his book is about in terms that everyone can understand. He reduces the plot, indeed its subject matter, to the barest essentials:

> Paludes . . . c'est l'histoire du terrain neutre, celui qui est à tout le monde . . . mieux: de l'homme normal, celui sur qui commence chacun—l'histoire de la troisième personne, celle dont on parle—qui vit en chacun, et qui ne meurt pas avec nous.—Dans Virgile il s'appelle Tityre—et il nous est dit expressément qu'il est *couché*—"*Tityre recubans.*"—Paludes, c'est l'histoire de l'homme couché.[20]

Subsequently the plot takes on more significance, the indications become more precise in his descriptions, but only as a result of direct questioning from people with specific orientations.

For the naturalist, the narrator of *Paludes* sees his book as the tale of animals whose eyes stop functioning because there is no need to see in the dark cave they have chosen as their home. For the moralist the book becomes a spur to action, although an imperfect one, because, as he observes, "you will not teach how to want: *velle non discitur.*"[21] An extremely significant revelation is prompted by Evariste, the subtle critic, who objects that *Paludes* is a bit special as a subject. "Art," its author replies, "is painting a particular subject with such force that the generality upon which it depends is comprehended."[22] Thus the relationship between the particular and the general, which was to occupy so much of Gide's time and writing in the following years, is here succinctly stated.[28] The process whereby a particular subject or theme is treated with sufficient vigor to reveal its generality involves the reduction of its diverse elements in reality to a single and consistent symbol. That is, the process requires a consistent adaptation and subordination of pretexts to theme. Thus, if we take happiness to be a warm puppy, Paradise would be a field filled with young canines, or Charity, the liberal distribution of puppies, and so on *ad absurdum*. Tityre and his swamp are the intense particularizations of the general notions, stagnancy and impotence. Because these are their only attributes and because all that happens in the course of the novel is made consistent with them, Tityre and his abode lose all reality. This particularization is dictated by aesthetic considerations ("la vérité du symbole") and results in the domination of a single trait that excludes or subordinates all other realistically plausible qualities, as in caricature. Because just one trait is dominant, no matter how particular a form it may take or how many transformations it may undergo, its persistence orients the reader's thinking and invites him to find hidden parallels in his own life.

The important and controlling element in this process, as suggested by Gide's protagonist, is the initial symbol of an emotion. After he has established his paludal image, everything in reality evoking a similar emotion is translated, if relevant and useful, into terms of that initial image. The image-symbol is an exteriorization of his emotion, but as an aesthetic unit it functions independently of him; moreover it also functions as an external influence upon him and, like tinted glasses, it colors his vision of the world. But this is aesthetically efficacious because the tinted glasses deform his vision in their own way, so that what he sees is readily converted into the language of the initial image. The narrator constantly carries a notebook in order to sketch on the spot what is "good for *Paludes.*"

The narrator offers an excellent example of this type of conversion in his treatment of Richard. We are even able to follow the process in detail. When he tests the effectiveness of his characterization of Tityre on his friend Hubert and fails, Richard appears with an inspiring tale of woe and joyous acceptance of all calamities. Richard's joy not only suits the novelist's conception of Tityre but inspires a detail strong enough, he hopes, to stir Hubert. Tityre, he later tells his difficult friend, is forbidden to eat the ducks he has killed, on the grounds that they would be injurious to his spiritual and mental health. Urged to follow the principles of homeopathic therapy, Tityre takes to eating slime worms. The very essence of the swamp is in these worms, thereby affording, by inoculation, a guard against any possible swamp disease. "But the surprising part is that Tityre tastes them; he becomes accustomed to them in a few days, and will eventually find them excellent." [24] Hubert remains unimpressed but the episode demonstrates how the narrator—and Gide, too—adjusts reality to fit what he deems "la vérité du symbole." To be sure, the slime worms are the narrator's own invention and stem from the revulsion Richard inspires in him; but it is significant that his reactions to Richard's acceptance take the form of an image that is entirely in keeping with the controlling swamp image.

In the rest of the letter written to Scheffer, Gide made the following suggestion concerning the isolation of "personality buds" in fiction:

A word of advice: choose preferably (if it is true that one can choose) the bud which disturbs you most. You get rid of it at the same time. [25]

Two Images

He put this precept into practice as early as *La Tentative amoureuse* and continued to do so in many of his subsequent works. This theory ironically does not hold for the imaginary author of *Paludes*, who was obviously too obsessed by his idea to purge himself through writing. But it did work for Gide himself. *Paludes* permitted him an outlet for his resentment against his stagnant Symbolist period [26] and freed him as well of his obsession with the swamp image. It never appears again in his fictional works, though it does crop up occasionally in his journals and correspondence to describe periods of depression. Previously it had appeared in *Les Poésies d'André Walter*, particularly in "Polders," and he had expanded it into the second landscape of *Le Voyage d'Urien*. But what distinguishes the image in these two works from *Paludes* is principally Gide's attitude towards it and consequently its behavior. Although in both cases the image symbolizes the same emotions, Gide approaches it, in the first two instances, quite seriously, but in *Paludes* he is amused and ironical. In "Polders" the poet is victim of the lethargy he sees in the landscape; in *Le Voyage*, Urien and his creator struggle to remain above its influence but see it with only a modest measure of objectivity; finally in *Paludes*, the hero is again victim of his landscape, but Gide is quite remote from the feelings expressed. Unlike his protagonist, he is subject to a different interior landscape that permits his image to function independently of his emotions.

The importance of *Paludes* in the development of Gide's attitude towards the image can be attributed to the effective execution of the theories Gide's narrator illustrates. At the source of these theories is the notion of a freely functioning and controlling image which, though fed by the author's emotions, remains independent of them. The discovery of the aesthetic efficacy of such an image can be traced to its first, though stunted, appearance in *La Tentative amoureuse*, to

97

the cuttlefish egg. But this image was remote from Gide's own feelings, whereas the emotions suggested by *Paludes* had been, at one time, particularly close to him. Gide's feelings must have undergone a great change in order to produce such a book as *Paludes*. The critical works Gide conceived and composed during the months he worked on *Paludes* and the period immediately following offer many insights into the nature of this change and its effect upon his concept of the image.

V

The Critical Works

Paludes was composed between the two halves of the most
critical period in Gide's life; that is, during his sojourn at
La Brévine (Neuchâtel), which followed his first voyage to
Africa and his first sensual experience and preceded his second voyage to Africa and the confirmation of his homosexual
proclivities. *Paludes,* conceived and executed in a wintry
Switzerland between states of extreme fervor, has been justly
considered an ironic tribute to the dead Symbolist episode
that began after the publication of *Les Cahiers d'André
Walter.* But the book does not so much close a period of
Gide's life as it points to another. Nearly everything of significance in *Paludes* looks ahead; what was resolved perhaps
only instinctively during the Neuchâtel sojourn forms the
substance of the numerous critical essays and lectures that followed continuously until the collapse of *L'Ermitage* in 1908
and that were later collected in *Prétextes* and *Nouveaux Prétextes.*

The book that vehemently negates his Symbolist past is *Les
Nourritures terrestres;* begun during the first trip to North
Africa and expanded during subsequent trips, it was finished
during the winter of 1896-1897 at La Roque. In the very title
Gide repudiates the values of his Symbolist period (and of his
ascetic past as well), for nothing was pushed away by the
Symbolists with as much horror as "the fruits of the earth." [1]

99

The break was not as sudden as has been frequently claimed, however. Gide had already begun to show impatience with the hothouse atmosphere of Parisian literary circles and, almost in the middle of writing *La Tentative amoureuse*, he began to evince an avid interest in this world. His reorientation was begun under the joint influence of the poetry of Francis Jammes (to whom *La Tentative* was dedicated), the companionship of Paul-Albert Laurens and his family, and the beauty of the Laurens' summer place at Yport. During his stay at Yport in the summer of 1893, Gide quickly became tired of his essay. He finished it hurriedly late that summer. Once acquitted of this debt to the past, he was free to interest himself in other things. In October, he and Paul-Albert Laurens left for Africa, both seeking a sensual renascence.

The emergence of a different attitude towards *La Tentative amoureuse* is apparent in the work itself and coincides with Gide's stay in Yport. Beyond any hope of profiting from Symbolism and impatient to enter into a new phase and a new mode of experience, Gide had great difficulty finishing this project, which he had begun earlier in Paris.[2] Only through the discipline aroused by a vague feeling of duty and virtue did he manage to bring the work to a conclusion. But the conclusion is noticeably hurried. At the beginning of Part Three, which lasts little over three pages, less than half the length of each of the two preceding sections, Gide bluntly expresses his wish to be done with autumn.

> Madam, this story bores me. . . . I wanted to describe a relationship between the seasons and the soul; we had to come to Autumn; I do not like to abandon any task I have undertaken.[3]

Part Four, which is still shorter and unnumbered, as though unnamed in the manner of an epilogue, roundly dispatches winter in a brief paragraph. The rest of the section is devoted to Gide's condemning the satisfaction of desire.

Gide was quite able to turn a fault or inadequacy into a virtue; and, in this case, to turn the psychological causes of an aesthetic failure into a working aesthetic principle and justification of the work. "I wanted to indicate, in this *Tentative amoureuse*," he wrote in his journal at the end of the summer of 1893, "the influence of the book on him who writes during the very process of writing it." [4] This is clearly a rationalization after the fact and not at all in accord with his intentions originally suggested by the book's preface and subtitle, "Le Traité du vain désir."

Evolving a work of art and gleaning aesthetic principles from its evolution, as Gide did for *La Tentative*, is a process similar to the one he used during and after the composition of *Paludes*. Much of the period between autumn, 1894, and the publication of *Les Nourritures terrestres* in 1897 was devoted to formulating aesthetic principles first arrived at during the late months of 1894 at Neuchâtel. These principles were apparently discovered through the very act of writing and under the influence of a particular state of mind. After the revelatory experiences of his first visit to Africa, Gide was unable to return to the life of his erstwhile Parisian associates, as earlier he had been unable to give himself entirely to the full realization of the intentions of *La Tentative*. In both cases his detachment betrays itself artistically through irony. His incapacity for certain types of involvement (in the earlier case, involvement in the already outgrown subject matter of his work and, in the later, involvement in a pattern of life already bypassed because of the intensity of new experiences) forms the ground-work for aesthetic development. Condemned because of ill-health to spend the winter at Neuchâtel, Gide found himself living in an emotional limbo, tensely anticipating the return to Africa and investing his hope in an imminent victory over Madeleine's resistance to his marriage proposals, yet feeling remote from his former pious and aesthetic self. In this frame of mind he conceived and executed *Paludes* and envisaged as well many of his other principal works.[5] His first African encounter and subsequent brush with death had the salutary effect of enabling him to interpose distance between his emotions and their aesthetic formulation and to objectify his emotional commitment to, and involvement in, a work of art.

The progress made by Gide during this period was not only aesthetic but emotional and intellectual as well. It was noted that one fault of *Les Cahiers d'André Walter* was its lack of reserve and analysis. Gide had tried to express himself, his adolescent problems, and preoccupations *in toto*, but without the benefit of order. After the literary debauch of *Les Cahiers* Gide slowly applied analysis—the surgery of reason—to his personality. Dividing his whole personality into little bundles of isolated tendencies benefited not only his psyche but also his literary output; for these isolated bundles were permitted unfettered development in Gide's various *récits*, *soties*, and *traités*. Through this kind of catharsis Gide saved himself the pains and painful results of the full development of any single one of his conflicting tendencies. He was ultimately able to reconcile the disparate elements of his personality and so attained a measure of harmony and serenity in his later years.

The period at Neuchâtel was devoted to the initial stages of this analysis. In a letter written to Pierre Louÿs in October, 1894, Gide complained that, despite the great amount of work he had been doing, there had been few concrete results. "I am going through a period," he continued, "which I think will decide my entire intellectual value . . . my thinking is becoming firm and orderly. . . . *I am connecting all my ideas.*" [6] Though this period of *recueillement* at La Brévine had both emotional and intellectual value, the intellectual results came first, because Gide could handle rational experience more easily and because only by reason, he felt, could he effectively direct his emotions. A preface written during the summer of 1895 for a second edition of *Paludes* provides the best available introduction to his thinking at the time. Speaking of himself in the third person, Gide states that because of a long voyage he had been able to set aside his books and break open the windows that had kept him from fresh air; finally harmonizing, he adds,

> sa vie et ses pensées, selon l'optimisme éperdu où l'avaient conduit son tempérament d'abord, puis son admiration pour Goethe et la lente méditation de Leibniz.[7]

The role played by temperament in his transformation has been treated most technically by the psychologist Jean Delay. Goethe's role has been discussed by Gide himself and more recently by Renée Lang in *André Gide et la pensée allemande*. The part played by Leibniz, however, seems to have been neglected or at best understated in critical literature.

In an article on the problems of influence in literature,[8] Henri Peyre has transcribed remarks made by Gide himself disclaiming any influence by Leibniz upon his own life and work. Peyre does not conjecture, on the basis of similar statements in *Si le Grain ne meurt*,[9] that these remarks were probably made only with the Leibniz of the *Theodicy* in mind. Renée Lang, too, seems to dismiss Leibniz and the possibility of his influence on Gide with hardly more than a paragraph.

> As for Leibniz, imbued with French culture, with his logical concepts and harmonious pantheism, he could have pleased the young man in revolt against the austere religion of his childhood. But here again, Gide seems to have relished primarily the gratuitous joy derived from effort.[10]

The gratuitous joy derived from effort does not, however, accord with Gide's stated "lente méditation." What he slowly meditated upon during his stay at La Brévine was one of Leibniz's less mystical works. The *Journal* provides us with its title, curiously omitted from the memoirs. Barely settled at Neuchâtel at the end of September, 1894, Gide made the following entry:

> I am going to take up Leibniz at the point where I had left him . . . at the moment I have begun the *Nouveaux Essais*.[11]

In several other entries for the month of October, 1894, he quotes and comments upon several lines from the *Nouveaux Essais*, and in a letter to Valéry dated November 11, 1894, he takes one of Leibniz's observations to its logical conclusion and applies it to himself:

> "Un état peut être volontaire sans être libre," dit, entre autres, Leibniz et c'est assez banal, mais ce qui ne l'est pas c'est de, contraint ou non, travailler à faire tous ses états *volontaires*. . . . Ma sagesse est là, je dis sagesse, puisqu'ainsi l'on nomme une recette de bonheur.[12]

Gide never openly paid tribute to the author of the *Nouveaux Essais*; yet one might interpret the enigmatic epigraph of *Paludes*, "*Dic cur hic* (l'autre école)," as a veiled acknowledgment of his debt to Leibniz. The Latin expression appears twice in the essays to characterize an attitude totally opposed to the one prevalent in *Paludes*. Leibniz urges us "to collect our thoughts and to raise ourselves above the present tumult of impressions, to go forth, so to speak, from the place where we are, to say to ourselves: '*Dic cur hic? respice finem*, where are we then? or let us come to the purpose, let us come to the point.' " [13] Of all the characters that appear in *Paludes*, the narrator alone is able to take stock of his situation in this manner. That he is unable to act, as a result, can be attributed to "la vérité du symbole," that is, to Gide. But this detail does not prevent him from deeming himself a member of "the other school." Gide was, at the time of *Paludes*, precisely in the frame of mind advocated by Leibniz.

The nature or depth of his thinking about the *Nouveaux Essais* may be, in the long run, no more than conjecture, but, as such, conjecture may fashion a point of view which in turn sheds light on fact. If, as Gide himself states at this same period, "in every relationship lies the possibility of influence," [14] a brief discussion of Leibniz's work will be necessary to clarify, if not define, the rapport between the two.

The complete title of the book in question is *Nouveaux Essais sur l'entendement humain.* It is very nearly a point-by-point consideration—at times, refutation—of Locke's *Essay Concerning Human Understanding.* The fundamental difference between the two epistemologists can perhaps be described as a difference in conception of human psychology. Because of this difference, Leibniz was led to accept what Locke bitterly condemned, the existence of innate ideas in the human psyche.

By defending the existence of innate ideas, Leibniz seems to take up the defense of Descartes as well. But he was unwilling to follow Descartes all the way since his definition of innate ideas is more modest and reflects a slightly different point of view. Rather than accept the Cartesian notion of a static psyche that receives all its ideas upon leaving the hands of the maker, Leibniz saw the importance of contingent and external phenomena to the knowledge-gathering process. He refused to go as far as Locke, however, in assigning to contingent phenomena (and to the senses which receive and record their impressions) an exclusive role in the knowledge-gathering activity; this objection occasioned the *Nouveaux Essais*. In reconciling what he saw as the virtues of the two antagonistic systems, Leibniz was obliged to scrutinize the meaning of knowledge and to distinguish its different types according to its sources. But, since knowledge rests upon ideas,[15] the sources of these ideas and the truths which depend upon them fell under his analysis. In his view human knowledge is composed of two kinds of truths, those of the understanding and those of fact. The first are entirely products of the mind, and are universal or, in Leibniz's terms, necessary, whereas the latter are products of the senses, the results of experience, and are contingent.

> The original proof of the necessary truths comes from the understanding alone, and the other truths come from experience or from the observation of the senses. Our mind is capable of knowing both; but it is the source of the former, and whatever number of particular experiences we may have of a universal truth, we could not be assured of it forever by induction without knowing its necessity through the reason. . . . The senses can hint at, justify, and confirm these truths, but cannot demonstrate their infallible and perpetual certainty.

These are the ideas or truths that Leibniz considers innate, that exist in the human psyche if not actually, at least virtually. But, as suggested above, real phenomena can hint at these truths. That is, Leibniz suggests a dynamism between mind and reality, between truths of necessity and truths of fact. In this way he leaves an opening for Locke.

> It is incontestable that the senses do not suffice to show [the] necessity [of universal truths], and that thus the mind has a disposition (active as well as passive) to draw

them to itself from its own depths; although the senses are necessary to give it the occasion and attention for this. . . .[16]

Thus Leibniz struck a middle path between Descartes and Locke, considering human knowledge as derived from both those aspects of the psyche that each of his predecessors propounded exclusively. Despite his insistence upon innate ideas—or rather, upon ideas which are of the understanding alone—Leibniz recognizes the catalytic effect that the senses have upon the understanding. He thereby acknowledges, unlike Descartes, the role of the outside world and of the body in the learning process.

It was probably these latter notions that first intrigued Gide, who had been wrestling with the problem of the importance of his own experience to ultimate reality. Leibniz underlined the importance of experience in the truth-gathering activity to a heretofore convinced Cartesian, who had expected to resolve the problems of reality by means of introspection. Through Leibniz, Gide discovered the philosophical justification of sense-experience in the formation of ideas. Absolute truth concerning man and his condition, which was Gide's main objective during his Symbolist period, is beyond the ken of man. Such truths belong only to God, he realized,[17] whereas ideas and truths derived from fact are the stock in trade of man, whose raw materials are generally the impulses received through the senses. The number and variety of impulses that the human mind can receive and assimilate are infinite; so too, then, are the ideas which they may evoke. Thus, if we follow this line of reasoning, the truths which reason extracts from such ideas are necessarily unlimited as well. It was precisely the inherited belief in a finite number of truths about man that Gide had to get rid of in preparation for the discovery of his "norm" and his final self-affirmation in January, 1895. For the belief in the supremacy of a fixed number of truths concerning human activity, imposed by God and placed in an Eden resembling the one described in *Le Traité du Narcisse*, would necessarily inhibit the faithful from "manifesting" any deviation, however authentic, from these truths. Gide's concern was human history, man and all his capabilities. He was seeking a definition of man that would include any deviation from the so-called cultural norms. But a definition of man would limit him, or our conception of him, by excluding what lies beyond the definition. Gide soon realized that man is essentially indefinable and that each individual, wondrous in his uniqueness, contributes to a working definition of what man is—or rather, what he has been so far and not at all what he should continue to be in the future.

There is, thus, no limit on truths about man; those already established cannot limit or prevent the revelation of new ones. Though cultures tend to limit or prevent such revelation by raising already revealed truths to the level of norms to be imitated, the affirmation of any deviation (whose presence in a human being is the handiwork of God) proves its validity. For Gide felt God does not tempt us beyond our powers of resistance. Since ultimate truth has its source in God alone, we can in time partially discover this truth by providing examples of its validity in as many different ways as possible, examples which we as humans can readily observe only through our senses. Here is, no doubt, the rational source of Gide's obsessive self-revelation.

These ideas, prompted in part by a careful reading of Leibniz's *Nouveaux Essais* and reflected periodically in the *Journal* during the last months of 1894, are the results of a long meditation, which bore fruit belatedly in *Réflexions sur quelques points de littérature et de morale*. Here many ideas gleaned from Leibniz are digested and placed in a context along with other ideas whose various sources are not relevant to our present purpose. The subject of the pamphlet is the inter-dependence of "littérature et morale," and the progression of the title from its original to its final form in the *Journal* (*Littérature et morale*) fuses the two essential elements into a closer harmony and dependence. Of these two elements it is literature that commands the more importance, if not, in fact, the more space. Only the last two pages are entirely devoted to "la théorie du livre," but the vocabulary there used, the concepts there alluded to, are the prime concern of the earlier and more numerous pages. The pamphlet is the statement of a point of view, of a way of seeing the world and its inhabitants and the artist's role in it. Although it would seem to cover the same ground as *Le Traité du Narcisse*, the two statements differ profoundly because of the different value each pamphlet attributes to immediate phenomena and because of the different role seen for the artist.

The three pivotal points considered here are art, reality, and the artist. Reality for the Narcissus-Poet, we recall from *Le Traité*, is no more than a confused and imperfect imitation of the ideal realms of Paradise; reality is made up of symbols of the archetypes they strive to be and to express. It is the Poet's task, then, to observe phenomena in the attempt to perceive archetypes. But unlike the scholar, who is seeking the same thing, the Poet intuits the archetypes of what he sees about him. He is a visionary who sees through the world of appearances to essential and ideal reality. Once he sees the archetype, he uses all the materials of his medium in the most effective way to create a beautiful and eternal garb for this idea. The end of his activity is the re-creation of a lost Paradise. Art, then, is an Olympus, the dwelling place of truths in a pure aesthetic form, above and beyond the ebb and flow of human time.

The conclusion of *Littérature et morale* describes a unique role for the artist.

Je soutiendrai qu'il faut ceci, pour un artiste: un monde spécial dont il ait seul la clef. Il ne suffit pas qu'il apporte une chose nouvelle, quoique cela soit énorme déjà; mais bien que toutes choses en lui soient ou semblent nouvelles, transapparues derrière une idiosyncrasie puissament coloratrice.

Il faut qu'il ait une philosophie, une esthétique, une morale particulières; toute son oeuvre ne tend qu'à le montrer. Et c'est ce qui fait son style. J'ai trouvé aussi, et c'est très important, qu'il lui faut une plaisanterie particulière; un drôle à lui.[18]

To his uniqueness is due the novel view of reality that he brings forth and that he expresses by his whole being. By developing this view the artist expresses an idea that enlarges upon the extant idea of man. Instead of discarding what does not coincide with already established truths, he affirms what is different, thus releasing a new truth. "Ne plus considérer en chaque être," Gide affirms in *Littérature et morale*, "que la part unique et différente, dont cette matière commune n'était que le trop massif soutien." [19] In this manner he obtains greater knowledge of himself and of the world about him.

Since Gide's objective in scrutinizing his interior landscape, as expressed in *Le Traité*, was to find in himself the archetypes of man, he had tended to shed all that had no precedent, all that was different, all that did not conform to the New Testament image of "the new man." Gide well knew at the time that this tendency could leave very little room for innovation in art as well as in conduct and was accordingly troubled by categorical denials of the new in art such as La Bruyère's. With *Littérature et morale*, he began to formulate an answer to this denial. Further developed in "Lettre à Angèle" ("Stevenson et du *Nationalisme en littéra-*

ture," May, 1899), "La Querelle du Peuplier" (1903), "Chroniques à *L'Ermitage*" (February, 1905), his answer was given final expression in the two major articles of 1909, "Nationalisme et littérature." Gide affirmed that all has not been said, that man is not confined to the image formed by the Hebraic-Christian legacy or even by the Graeco-Roman tradition. These are but two ideas evolved of and by man, but by no means the only valid ones. In a chronicle to *L'Ermitage*, Gide refutes the arguments of an imaginary interviewer who denies the new by invoking Solomon of Ecclesiastes and also La Bruyère. He defends the therapeutic effect of "les mauvaises fréquentations" upon the restricted culture that produced La Bruyère.

> Du bien vivre et du bien penser, on avait trouvé la recette. Nous avions hérité des Latins une image de l'homme juste, belle, modèle d'après lequel nous nous étions formés, sans avoir pu d'abord nous aviser que ne s'y épuisait peut-être pas complètement notre essence: il semblait qu'on dût s'y tenir. . . . De l'étranger on n'acceptait rien que ce qui rappelait cette image. . . . Eh! parbleu oui! Tout était dit, depuis les sept mille ans qu'il y avait des hommes, et "qui pensent"—mais depuis les gouffres d'années qu'il y avait des brutes et *qui ne pensent pas*—qui n'avaient pas encore pensé, que de choses restaient à dire! [20]

The major point made in this debate of 1905 is that the essence of the French national character, if there be any, has not yet been fully expressed by any one national image, nor indeed can it ever be so fully expressed and defined, unless France should cease to exist. So long as a culture remains alive, its outer limits are constantly being widened by those strong enough to outgrow the image it tries to impose. And, by extension, so long as man remains, his essence is enriched precisely by those "deviants" in any given culture.[21]

But to affirm one's difference against generally accepted behavior is extremely difficult. Societies tend to impose conformity by denying any variant of its own image. This is an error, Gide says. First, it is wrong to condemn anything human, however foreign it is to one's own ideas. The correct formula, Gide asserted during those important months of late 1894, is "to take upon oneself as much humanity as possible";[22] and he repeats this idea in *Littérature et morale*, this time in imitation of Terence's Latin: *Nil humanum a me alienum puto.*[23] Secondly, it is an error in that it sins against nature; man can never successfully suppress anything human. "There is never a definitive victory in the world of morality," Gide says, early in the pamphlet. This affirmation runs through the journal entries of late 1894. To oppose Nature,

> cela peut bien flatter l'orgueil et servir à la poésie; mais cela n'est pas *raisonnable*. Une claire entente de Dieu fait souhaiter d'aller dans le sens des choses, dans le sens de soi-même. . . . Les lois de la nature sont celles de Dieu . . . elles sont en nous. . . . L'homme qui s'y soumet volontiers est le sage; la nature y soumet les fous.[24]

The moral lesson implicit here in *Littérature et morale* repeats that of *Le Traité* in that both affirm "we live in order to manifest," "we have only a representative value."[25] These words, "manifester" and "représenter" seem to mean the same thing and are nearly interchangeable. Gide, however, had a predilection for the word "représenter" after 1895.[26] The change in vocabulary can be attributed to a desire on Gide's part to avoid the mystical and revelatory connotation of "manifester"; he preferred the alternative, with none of the flavor of biblical language about it. The word "représenter" in Gide's usage seems to carry with it more the feeling of calling into being something that has not before existed, whereas the term "manifester" suggests rendering palpable something that has existed and still continues to exist but elsewhere and in a different and eternal form. This distinction is useful in confronting the two essays because, first, it underlines the nature of the objects acted upon, what is manifested, what is represented; and, secondly, it permits us a glimpse into the heart of the poetic vision of each essay.

Gide tells us in *Le Traité* that the Poet, by seizing the idea behind the Maian veil and giving it permanent expression in art, makes palpable something that exists, if only ideally, and whose traces are obscured by contingency. In the later manifesto, it is again a question of the Idea, but here it is not to be confused with Truth. In the important entries to the journal of 1894, Gide cites Leibniz on several occasions precisely in order to distinguish between the two terms. Truths, he decided then, are the inhabitants of Olympus and are the Ideas in the Platonic sense of *Le Traité*. But they are not an exclusive set since their numbers can be increased infinitely. Ideas, in their new sense, are not absolutes but merely perceived relationships, or, metaphorically, "the refraction of an effective relationship in the mind of man." [27] As such they are the source of truths [28] and they attain this level by being affirmed, by being "played out." It is in this sense that one may understand Gide's statement that "an idea is the temptation of its truth" [29] as well as the important, even key, phrase at the center of *Littérature et morale*: "the history of man is the history of the truths which he has released." [30] The ensuing discussion, which this statement introduces, expands this idea and ends with the following remarks:

Le temps et l'espace sont les tréteaux que, pour s'y jouer, les innombrables vérités ont déployés à l'aide de nos cerveaux, et nous y jouons comme des marionnettes volontaires, convaincues, dévouées et voluptueuses. Je ne vois pas qu'il y ait là de quoi s'attrister; je me plais au contraire à cette conviction de mon rôle, et ce rôle, somme toute, si tout le motive, c'est bien un chacun seul qui l'invente.[31]

Immediately following, Gide adds: "You will learn to consider humanity as the staging of ideas on earth. We have only a representative value."

Gide no longer sought exaltation, as did André Walter, in a rigorous conformity to an image of man that has been spent. His need to exalt and exult found outlet in his own uniqueness, in the new idea he felt himself called upon to express, and in the knowledge that he no longer deemed himself superior to the idea he felt obliged to represent. Thus, the conclusion of the pamphlet suggests, Gide found in his own difference and in the difficulty of expressing it the source of his artistic inspiration.

The manifesto, *Littérature et morale,* in defending the artist's uniqueness, explores its utility for literary production. But this defense and exploration do not fully satisfy the double subject-heading of the title. It is only in the final section, devoted entirely to the theory of art, that this full satisfaction comes. Here Gide pauses to discuss the essence of a work of art: its composition. To be sure, this discussion is extremely brief and cryptic; it was the style he chose for the pamphlet. Nevertheless these sparse entries go beyond the simplicity of generalities because of the vocabulary used and because of the direction and unity of purpose given the entire work in the concluding paragraphs, here cited *in toto:*

En étudiant la question de la raison d'être de l'oeuvre d'art, on arrive à trouver que cette raison suffisante, ce symbole de l'oeuvre, c'est sa composition. Une oeuvre bien composée est nécessairement symbolique. Autour de quoi viendraient se grouper les parties? qui guiderait leur ordonnance? sinon l'idée de l'oeuvre, qui fait cette ordonnance symbolique. L'oeuvre d'art, c'est une idée qu'on exagère. Le symbole, c'est autour de quoi se compose un livre. La phrase est une excroissance de l'idée. THÉORIE. Les choses sont perpétuellement en inéquilibre; de là leur écoulement. L'équilibre, c'est la "santé" parfaite; ce que M. Taine appelle un accident heureux; mais il est irréalisable physiquement à cause de ce que nous disions; réalisable seulement dans l'oeuvre d'art. L'oeuvre d'art est un équilibre hors du temps, une santé artificielle.[32]

The mere existence of a work of art without any obvious purpose or function must have troubled Gide as soon as he began devoting himself seriously to literature. What purpose could a work of pure lyricism possibly serve in the mind of the utilitarian-minded young Protestant that Gide was? As he said later, the aspect of literature that most interested him was also the least able to yield a valid self-justification to the most exacting of Protestants.[33] This same problem crops up in two other places in Gide's early writings, both at approximately the same time, during the period of *Le Traité du Narcisse*. In a letter to Paul Valéry dated June 17, 1891, Gide raises the question, why should there be such things as books? The tentative answer offered Valéry resembles the answer given in the coda of *Le Traité*. The justification of the "book" as it presented itself to Gide at this time was not only love, or sympathy, but "apostolic love"; [34] that is, the spreading of an evangel so that others will adore the beauties of the temple. Since everything has already been said,[35] the aim of his book is basically inspirational, the communication of enthusiasm, an aim only to be satisfied, it is implied, by the skill of the artist. Thus Gide, along with La Bruyère, saw the justification of the work of art in its artistry, in its purity of style—in a word, in its composition.

In this justification of art, both essays are in accord. *Le Traité du Narcisse*, however, insists less upon composition than upon inspiration, that is, the perception of the Idea to be composed. The later essay introduces a new understanding of "idea," as we have seen, and elevates it to a role equal in importance to "composition." Unlike *Le Traité*, *Littérature et morale* denies that all has been said and requires that the idea be both new and well-composed to justify a work's existence. But what precisely does Gide mean by "composition"?

In trying to order the cryptic remarks about art in the context of the entire pamphlet, one arrives at this basic axiom: "l'oeuvre d'art, c'est une idée qu'on exagère." The idea in question is no doubt of the same order discussed earlier in the pamphlet: the perception of a relationship. "Exagérer," however, requires closer scrutiny. The verb means "to overdo, magnify, overstep normal limits," primarily by speech. This can be done either by overstating the idea itself or by overstating its importance. The mechanics of the latter case may simply involve suppressing the usual and ordinary life-context of an idea, by ignoring the terrain which gave it life, or by simplifying an idea to the point of generalization. "To simplify is to exaggerate what remains," [36] Gide affirmed quite early in his journal. But surely this does not exhaust the meaning of "exagérer." One may continue exaggerating an isolated idea by ordering its elements into a dynamic relationship, by molding it into a scenario, and finally by letting it grow independently into an organism. This is precisely the procedure

Gide seems to have followed in creating his fiction, and the genesis of *Paludes* offers its first illustration. Although *Paludes* was not composed until the fall of 1894, the idea of the work came to Gide as early as April, 1893. In an unpublished page of his journal he made the following entry:

> Elle avait peur de la volupté comme d'une chose trop forte et qui l'aurait pu tuer. Je vous assure que c'est une terreur, *comme celle de la mort.*

Gide prefaced this brief statement by a tentative title for the projected work: *Angèle ou le pauvre petit voyage.*[37] The work thus began taking form, although not the final form that we know today. If we conjecture the original idea of the work as "menacing sensuality," we have all the elements of the process described above. The idea composed into the description of a protagonist dominated by it and who expresses it in and through a definite situation—a paltry trip—is the "exaggerated" idea, or the scenario, of the work. One more illustration of this process will suffice to establish it as a definite procedural device of Gide's. In the *Feuillets* of 1897-1902, Gide made the following entry under the rubric *Petit Roman*:

> Sensualité précipitée.
> (Sa précipitation était telle, qu'il s'écorchait les mains aux serrures.) [38]

This is certainly a prefiguration of *L'Immoraliste*, which was not published until 1902.[39]

Once the work of art has reached the stages outlined above, there remains only the final and most difficult stage, that of "imagination."

Pour moi, l'idée d'une oeuvre précède souvent de plusieurs années son *imagination*.

Dès que l'idée d'une oeuvre a pris corps, j'entends: dès que cette oeuvre s'organise, l'élaboration ne consiste guère qu'à supprimer tout ce qui est inutile à son *organisme*.[40]

It is pertinent to note here the literal meaning of the verb "organiser"; in the light of the context it might have been just as accurately rendered by "se fait organisme." It is well known that Gide frequently borrowed terms from the natural sciences to describe his artistic method. Here the use of such terminology serves to clarify his understanding of "imagination." The word is used to denote the process whereby an idea is put into image form, that is, into a concrete situation. This stage is illustrated by the final form of the work, the journal in *Paludes*, Michel's narrative, Alissa's and Jérôme's account of their relationship.

The relationship between the idea of a work and its composition still remains to be clarified. If composition means, as we contend, the initial ordering of an idea into a dynamic form resulting in a scenario of the work, then this ordering may be considered the idea's first configuration or, as Gide states, its symbol. The justification for this assertion may be seen in the fact that the "composition" appears to be (in Gide's mind) equidistant from the idea and the full "exagération" or "imagination" of the work. The meaning of symbol here is literal: a concrete sign for something abstract, the idea, on the one hand, as well as the succinct representative of something larger and more diffuse—the completed work of art—on the other. The symbol of the work of art entitled *L'Immoraliste* is the scenario suggested above: "Sa précipitation était telle, qu'il s'écorchait les mains aux serrures." This first image of the work does not occur at all in the novel yet it does give the essence of the "récit." Michel spent the first part of his life ignoring or repudiating his innate penchant for sensual experience; yet once he does experience the joy of sensuality, he becomes so intoxicated with his sensations that he prepares to abandon, indeed, sacrifice, all else to it; at the end, he destroys any hope of equilibrium while barely on the threshold of complete hedonism.

Thus, when Gide says that a well-composed book is necessarily symbolical and that it is the idea of the work that makes the ordering of its parts symbolical, he implies that the work of art is the particularization of an abstract, disembodied idea, yet so ordered that it is independent of and no longer directly motivated by the idea. This notion becomes clearer and more explicit in a later essay published in *L'Ermitage* (1898), in the first of his *Lettres à Angèle*. Speaking of the plays of François de Curel, he reproaches them for being subordinated to the exposition of ideas.

The dramatic error is that the idea becomes more important in itself than the character that expresses it. Ideas should be expressed only by *action*—or, in other words, there should not be any ideas; or, in still other words, an *idea*, in the theatre, should be a character, a situation; the pseudo-ideas which are put in the mouths of characters are never anything more than opinions and must be subordinated to the characters; it is not through them primarily that the characters express themselves; ideas should only be the conscious content of their acts. The unconscious prop which is stronger, more interesting, more important, is the character himself.[41]

Although Gide's remarks were made with reference to the theatre, they apply as well to the novel; for in neither should the artist's preoccupation be the exposition of ideas so much as their demonstration. The fault with Curel's plays lies in the absence of subordination of his idea to the vehicle, in the too rapid "imagination" of his idea; in a word, the fault lies in its lack of composition. Like Gide, Curel begins with an idea; but he does not let it mature, he does not let it compose itself and take on its own body. What results is the frequent appearance of the author's hand in the work; its various elements tend to be imposed by him rather than dictated by the work itself. Moreover, the entire exposition of the idea lies in the conscious expression—verbal and dramatic—of the characters, so that the author has to juggle situations to facilitate this conscious expression. In the well-ordered work, however, the idea is demonstrated by the total expression—conscious or unconscious—of the characters, whose only motivation comes from within themselves. What is essential for the work of art, as Gide learned while writing *Paludes*, is the aesthetic distance from the work that the author must assume: this distance is implicit in "composition." In the *Feuillets* of 1921, Gide repeats an idea already suggested in the *Feuillets* of 1893.

> I feel that the composition of a book is of prime importance. . . . The best thing is to let a work compose and order itself alone, and above all not to *force* it.[42]

The most important discovery Gide made at La Brévine, which he later formulated and generalized in *Littérature et morale*, is the efficacy of "composition" in the meaning of the term outlined above: the working of an idea into an autonomous organism. He apparently stumbled upon it because he was psychologically unable to identify himself with the emotions to be portrayed in *Paludes*. The idea of the work, which we might properly identify as "immobilité précipitée," was freed from his emotional grip and was permitted to grow according to its own logic and not according to the requirements of Gide's ever-present and hovering emotion. In his first "Lettre à Angèle," Gide rigorously reproaches his imaginary correspondent for the very same faults as those of his early works.

> People around you condemn plots and dream of narratives without events. It is unfortunate; you used to be skilled at plots but in your book there is no longer a shadow of one. One goes through it as through an open field. . . . Don't push me on, dear Angèle, otherwise I'll end by saying that nothing interests me in a book except the revelation of a new attitude towards life.[43]

This last statement is, of course, an exaggeration, and Gide is quick to admit it. But it does contain a measure of truth if we consider it as applying to his own works. For in the conclusion of this brief discussion of Angèle's novel, Gide restates the terminal point of *Littérature et morale*:

> I should like to find in the work of an artist a special philosophy, a special ethics, a special language, a special sense of humor.[44]

Gide wished to see in a work of art a complete microcosm, entirely strange and complex as life itself. It is a microcosm because it is independent, without any visible external motivation and sufficient to itself; it is "strange" because in it the artist embodies a vision of the world peculiar to himself. Not that each individual work depicts the total vision of the artist, but rather that each work, whatever its idea, is produced from the vantage point of this total vision and thereby reflects it. Thus all that his work contains appears new because of his own distinct outlook. It is his personal philosophy that constitutes the individuality of the artist, that constitutes his idiosyncrasy.

"Idiosyncrasy" is another key word in *Littérature et morale*. Rather than just "individuality," it connotes "aberration" or "irregularity"; that is, it has an unsavory flavor because the individuality expressed lies outside the tenets of normal behavior. It is true that during Gide's Symbolist phase he affected certain mannerisms and styles of dress in order to distinguish himself as an artist. But this was a superficial distinctiveness. It was not until after his first trip to Africa, during the crucial months at La Brévine, that he saw the value of first accepting and then affirming his profound idiosyncrasy. I do not intend to limit Gide's idiosyncrasy to his homosexuality, although the two are surely intimately intertwined, but rather to see it in terms of his whole personality. In the letters he wrote from La Brévine, he affirmed his independence, his deep conviction of his role as artist, and his conception of this role. For the first time in his life, he seemed to accept, even choose, the complexity of his nature.

The courage to accept his difference and his determination to be different came, in part, from the long and slow meditation upon Leibniz's *Nouveaux Essais*. What in this work seems to have most impressed Gide was the distinction made between "truth" and "idea." This distinction had pertinent moral implications, since it opened the door to further exploration of what man can do and be. No longer limited to a belief in a fixed number of truths concerning man and controlling his behavior, Gide felt free to test and express new ideas. No longer concerned with the archetype of man, he sought precisely what made each man different from all others. So, too, in each object, it was its uniqueness that intrigued him and enlarged his experience. In the final analysis, his newly found point of view was to profit his own experience and, ultimately, of course, "l'oeuvre." "Take upon oneself as much humanity as possible," he said late in 1894, an assertion that underlies not only *Littérature et morale* but also *Les Nourritures terrestres* and most of his subsequent thinking.[45]

One cannot help conjecturing that, at the height of his fervor and thirst for experience, Gide might have approved the Leibnizian cliché that what is, is good. It was not until much later that he saw the dangers of "sensualité précipitée" and withdrew to the opposite pole in *L'Immoraliste, Saül,* and *El Hadj.* But such oscillation is part of experience too.

VI

The Keyhole Metaphor
and the Parable

Gide came to posit, in the "monde moral," the absence of
Absolute Truth: a human truth is merely an idea already expressed and generally accepted by society. The history of the
past is the history of all the truths which man has released,
Gide said both in the journal of 1894 and in *Littérature et
morale.* But he was no longer interested in these truths; he
had given up the past as the sole source of information concerning human conduct, for it yields only what man has been.
Dazzled by the image of future man that he glimpsed, Gide
was more concerned with realizing at least part of this image.
Complaining of our human failing, which fixes our gaze upon
the past, he admitted in *Littérature et morale*:

> I . . . do not understand why confidence in the beauty
> of the future does not prevail over adoration of the past.

Again referring to the past, Gide clarified his attitudes by a
later remark in the same essay: "Those relationships which
have been effected constitute the history of the past. That is
an accomplished fact and, for better or worse, there is no
going back; one could not do so anyway." [1]
Man's potential is realized only through the efforts of the

exceptional man; it is he who gives life to his idea, whatever it may be, by representing it and thus rendering perceptible a new relationship of the elements that compose man. An analysis of the exceptional man, as Gide saw him, is not in order here, but a few remarks will characterize him. His idiosyncrasy is not posited in him: it is potential, developed through experience, and expressed in action. Though he does not express all he is capable of in deeds, lest he limit himself and his possible future experience, he expresses his potential in another form of action, the work of art. Gide took Goethe as an example of this figure. In *Littérature et morale*, he quoted Goethe's affirmation that there were no crimes that he did not feel himself capable of committing. And yet he committed none of them, Gide observes.

> The greatest intelligences are also those most capable of great crimes, which ordinarily they do not commit out of wisdom and love and because they would be limited by them.[2]

The point is that he is capable of such actions, for only thus can he understand them and man as well; we understand only what we are capable of doing, he says on an earlier page of the pamphlet. It is in the interest of furthering his understanding of what man is and can do that the exceptional man explores what he himself can do. With an image recalling the harmonics of *Les Cahiers*, Gide suggests a consistent character trait of his own which he sees as an essential element of this figure: sympathy.[3] In a journal entry of December, 1908, Gide equated absence of sympathy with lack of imagination, concluding that the richest personalities are also perhaps the most sensitive;[4] and again in *Le Journal des Faux-Monnayeurs*, he saw in his aptitude for sympathy the key to his character as well as to his work. Because of this quality, he was able to

speak authentically from the point of view of the most disparate personalities, such as Lafcadio and Alissa.[5]

But if the artist experiments with certain ideas only in art,
to avoid the limiting consequences that would result in reality,
he cannot guarantee the same circumspection on the part of
his audience.[6] The danger of too lucid and too easily assimilated an idea is the point Gide made in the following journal
entry of late 1894:

> Il n'est pas bon de tenter les autres; Dieu envoie à chacun
> des tentations selon sa force; il est mal et peu sage de leur
> en fournir qu'ils ne puissent pas surmonter. Voilà pour-
> quoi l'instruction maladroite est redoutable; pourquoi il
> ne faut pas crier trop haut ses idées, de peur qu'un faible
> ne vous entende.
>
> La vérité peut être dite à tous; l'idée proportionnelle-
> ment aux forces de chacun.[7]

There exists a possibility of influence in any relationship,
Gide concludes the entry. It was not until several years later,
in 1900, that he expanded his ideas concerning influence. In
the lecture, "De l'Influence en littérature," he accepted as a
condition of greatness the possibility, even the need, of exert-
ing "bad" influence. "I do not at all mean that I approve of
that; I am only saying that without it, the great man is hardly
possible." [8] Moreover, he affirms, influence does not create, it
awakens; we are influenced only by what is, or becomes, important to us. Nevertheless the artist is tormented by the importance of his idea, to and for which he feels acutely responsible. This responsibility complicates the already difficult task
of expressing it in a medium foreign to it and not yet molded
to contain it. How, then, did Gide resolve the problem of expressing an idea with intensity and fullness while, at the same

time, offering enough for everyone to assimilate and profit from to his own capacity?

Gide's solution to this problem is suggested by two successive passages of *Littérature et morale*; the first deals with self-analysis, the second, with individualism.

> La synthèse doit se précéder d'analyse; et l'analyse, besoin de l'esprit, naît du sentiment de la complexité. Le sentiment de la complexité peut devenir une stupéfaction passionnée.[9]

The chief accomplishment of *Paludes* and of the period during which this book was composed was essentially Gide's discovery and application of self-analysis as absolutely necessary for the health of his work and personality. He had to find and define his idiosyncrasy in the context of a broad experience of the world and of himself in it. In *Paludes* he isolated one emotional reaction, simplified it, and composed it into an organized work of art. Having overcome the fear of sensual experience facilitated his treatment of this theme in *Paludes*, but it was nonetheless close enough to inspire feelings stronger than indifference yet weaker than hatred; he handled it with irony.

It was undoubtedly his idiosyncrasy that caused him to react to the world as he did; but it was his conscious and deliberate analysis that singled out this one of many reactions he had and that elevated it by simplification to the level of generality. This observation introduces the other entry to *Littérature et morale* mentioned earlier.

> Les caractères individuels sont plus généraux (j'entends: plus humains) que les caractères ethniques. Il faut comprendre: l'homme en tant qu'individu tente d'échapper à

la race. Et sitôt qu'il ne représente plus la race, il représente l'homme; l'idiosyncrasie est prétexte à généralités.[10]

Since the exceptional man's duty is to bring forth a new idea of man, he must isolate it from other ideas within himself and permit it to develop freely in a work of art. For only thus can it be easily perceived by all. The artist, we recall from *Paludes*, must depict a particular subject with such skill that the general truth upon which it depends can be clearly comprehended. Gide's narrator goes on to clarify this thought by resorting to a metaphor:

vous me comprendrez assurément en songeant à tout l'énorme paysage qui passe à travers le trou d'une serrure dès que l'oeil se rapproche suffisament de la porte. Tel, qui ne voit ici qu'une serrure, verrait le monde entier au travers s'il savait seulement se pencher. Il suffit qu'il y ait possibilité de généralisation; la généralisation, c'est au lecteur, au critique de la faire.[11]

This paragraph admirably synthesizes the theory and the aesthetic achievement of *Paludes*. The image of the keyhole as a metaphorical description of Gidian fiction contains the heart of the Neuchâtel discoveries.

In order to facilitate generalization, Gide further simplified his initial idea and scenario for *Angèle ou le pauvre petit voyage*. He transformed menacing sensuality and the voyage to a neighborhood park into immobility and the joys of vegetation. Gide's final metaphors then came naturally: the swamp, *Paludes*' central image, "Tityre *recubans*," its idea, and Tityre recumbent in the swamp and increasingly enjoying it, its scenario.

But Gide's *Paludes* is much more than the Tityre story, more than his narrator's *Paludes* and *Polders* taken together.

The Keyhole Metaphor and the Parable

Unlike many of Gide's later works, *Paludes* absorbs the scenario into its own fabric by the technique Gide identified as "en abyme." Previously used in *Les Cahiers d'André Walter*, *Le Traité du Narcisse*, and *La Tentative amoureuse*, and not again until *Les Faux-Monnayeurs*, this technique was formulated in the summer of 1893. He borrowed the term from heraldry, where it signifies placing a figure or a reproduction of the coat of arms itself at the center of the field. In the *Journal*, he stated his predilection for this device as he saw it transposed in painting and literature:

> In a work of art I rather like rediscovering the subject itself transposed on the scale of its characters. Nothing better clarifies and more surely establishes the proportions of the whole.

The Tityre story functions in *Paludes* in a similar manner: like the small convex mirror in the paintings of Memling, it reflects "in its turn the interior of the room in which the depicted scene is taking place." [12] But it goes further, for it tends to deform the reader's view of his own world as well. If the central or, metaphorically, the "keyhole," figure of the "sotie" is Tityre in his lair, and the title *Paludes* seems to support this view, Gide is the first to make generalizations of his subject by underlining its traits in the world of the narrator; in so doing he invites us to do the same.

Gide then creates the possibility of generalization by obliging his protagonist to see paludal traits in the world about him and finally by forcing him to see himself as victim of these very same traits. We need only follow Gide's example and seek out Tityre in our own midst. The critics of the time were not misled by this device. "*Paludes* touches upon what makes us suffer," [13] said Camille Mauclair, and, in an undated letter written to Gide probably at the same time, he went further in his appreciation of the book:

> Finally, I like *Paludes* because one has the feeling that you are really fed up, that you need some air, and these past few days I have seen all my friends startled by that, and I, too, am fed up and they all bore me and I would like to get away. The whole book is exquisite and instructive, like an indecency.[14]

Had Gide chosen to restrict his work to the Tityre story alone, the reader would have been obliged to make the first step in the direction of generalization on his own. This first step is not a great one to ask of a reader, for only by discovering a hidden meaning could he explain the author's insistence upon so special a subject. Less timid in his later works, Gide dispensed with this first step entirely and concentrated his efforts upon the elaboration of his special subject. In *Le Prométhée mal enchaîné*, *Philoctète*, *Le Roi Candaule*, and *Saül*, Gide concerns himself only with the "keyhole" figures. Yet, again, in the preface to *Le Roi Candaule*, he felt it necessary to reiterate his hopes and intentions as well as suggest possible generalizations for his play.

> Let no one see "symbols" here, but simply an invitation to generalize. And let the choice of such a subject, of the exceptional character of Candaule, find its explanation and its excuse in this invitation.[15]

But generalization is encouraged not only by the particular functioning in a general context but also by some of its own special qualities. The particular in *Paludes* is, of course, Tityre happily reconciled to his swamp. But as a human being totally dominated by one single trait, by his idiosyncrasy, he is unreal and implausible; he lives and functions in a world alien to our own. Still, he is a human being, whose force lies in the strength of his idiosyncrasy. This is precisely the state of affairs that the fictional author of *Paludes* described in his rebuttal of Evariste's objections; for generalization is forthcoming if the particular is painted with sufficient intensity. The justification of this intensity lies only in Tityre's being a pretext for generalization, and the reader's awareness of this fact prompts him to suspend his disbelief in Tityre's plausibility as a real human being.

Because of this intensity and implausibility, Tityre belongs to another realm, the artificial one of art and poetry; he has a classical pedigree, he is the product of another age and culture. The narrator, on the other hand, is a somewhat diluted version of Tityre; as such, he is more easily recognized than his prototype and functions in a more plausible context, the modern world. By juxtaposing these two figures, separable not only by their varying degrees of intensity but by their cultural backgrounds, Gide reinforces his invitation to generalize. The juxtaposition of Virgil's Tityrus, the narrator's unlikely but more modern society, and the world of the reader produces the shock of anachronism which elevates Tityre's idiosyncrasy beyond an ethnic or historical to a more general human level.

The temporal distance a work of art places between the figures it depicts and their audience was discussed by Racine in his preface to *Bajazet*. Here, in order to excuse his choice of a contemporary subject, Racine stated that spatial distance can substitute for temporal distance in order to obtain the same end: respect for the tragic hero, which is not normally forthcoming if he is viewed by the spectators in the same way they see their own contemporaries. In his lecture of 1904, entitled "L'Evolution du théâtre," Gide further analyzes the nature of this "respect" and the mechanism of "dépaysement" which yields it.

> An artist's choice of figures distant from us arises from the fact that time—or whatever distance is in question—gives us an image already shorn of the episodic, the bizarre, the ephemeral; it conserves only the core of profound truth upon which art can work.[16]

The truth in question is, of course, the idea perceived by the artist and is the standard about which the work is composed. Gide here echoes the narrator's discussion with Angèle concerning the opposition between psychological and realistic truth.[17] Anachronism and "dépaysement" free the artist from concern with realistic truth so as to portray forcefully psychological truth; they free the spectators, too, from the distraction of a familiar world, enabling them to concentrate upon the artist's particularization of a truth which they can then extend more easily to themselves.

Anachronism for the sake of prompting generalizations is a technique Gide used in many of the works that followed *Paludes.* The "en abyme" device, which aids the juxtaposition of different historical and cultural periods, is by no means limited to this function nor is it the only device available to fulfill it. Gide temporarily gave up the use of this device in favor of more subtle means to accomplish the same end. In *Le Prométhée mal enchaîné,* the classical and modern worlds are fused: Prometheus and his classical partners play out their roles in a contemporary Paris. In other mythological works, modern expressions and vocabulary, references to contemporary events and ideas are employed. In still others, such as *Philoctète* and *Le Roi Candaule,* anachronism is not stated but implied, thus leaving the reader the responsibility of generalizing.

Virgil's Tityrus was thus a happy find for Gide, not only because he served, by means of his idiosyncrasy, as a pretext for generalization applicable to Gide and his period, but also because he opened for exploitation the figures of another culture, who by their presence in a twentieth-century work of art could elevate it to a more general, human plane. Gide was thus drawn to the classical myths becaused they facilitated comprehension of what he had to say in a manner in keeping with it. Fully conscious of their efficacy while writing *Paludes*, he conceived of two new mythical works in addition to *Les Nourritures terrestres* and mentioned them in letters to Marcel Drouin and Pierre Louÿs.[18] *Philoctète* was published in 1899; fragments of *Proserpine* not until 1912. Most of Gide's mythical and classical works, moreover, were written in the years immediately following *Paludes*; only three date from the latter part of his life: *Oedipe* (1931), *Perséphone* (1934), which is a reworking of the earlier *Proserpine*, and *Thésée* (1946). His interest in classical mythology nevertheless remained constant throughout his life. Frequent allusions and references to the myths in his journals, letters, and articles, a long projected treatise on the subject, which yielded the fragment "Considérations sur la mythologie grecque," [19] bear testimony to his continual interest in, if not utilization of, the myths.

Gide's attachment to the legends seems to go beyond the aesthetic advantages outlined above. What more did they offer him? One might acknowledge that for Gide the Greek myths contained the wisdom of the ages in poetic garb. But it would be more accurate to say that Gide considered and treated them as fertile points of departure. He did not feel that the Greeks had exhausted the image of man in the myths they left us or that the myths represent those eternal truths which may legitimately exert a despotic control over us. They contain wisdom simply because their authors and audiences took into account the totality of *their* age.

Their wisdom, so highly prized by Gide, consisted of a profound understanding "of harmony of the individual, of the customs, of the city." [20] Whether their instinctive need for harmony gave rise to their tolerance of diversity or arose from it, Gide was loath to conjecture. Diversity, in any case, was prevalent and existed authentically and harmoniously.

L'être ne se banalisait pas, par contrainte, mais se poussait à bout, par vertu; chacun n'exigeait de soi que soi-même, et s'apposait, sans se déformer, sur le dieu. De là le grand nombre de dieux; aussi nombreux que les instincts des hommes. . . . La religion, pour eux, ne dressait pas, au sommet d'une croix ou sur terre, devant eux, tel faisceau de vertus, tel fantôme moral auquel il importât de ressembler, sous peine d'être tenu pour impie; l'homme type n'était pas un, mais légion; ou plutôt: il n'y avait pas d'homme type.

In conclusion to these remarks in "L'Évolution du théâtre," Gide affirmed that "paganism was, at the same time, the triumph of individualism and the conviction that man cannot make himself other than he is." [21] With the triumph of the individual and the divinization of all the instincts, the Greeks left to posterity an image of harmony and serenity. It becomes clear that Gide's attachment to the Greek heritage was based on the example and authorization it provided for him to follow his instincts and maintain a balance and harmony among them. But, more important for Gide's work, the Greeks also left in their myths an extremely rich source of ready-made distillations of various human experiences. The myths opened for exploration a mine of images into which he could infuse his own understanding by reworking them to make them relevant to his own purpose. Moreover, because these images were already distillates they suited Gide's own psychological needs for self-analysis. "I lived on the Bible and the Greek myths," he said in an interview with Léon Pierre-Quint. "In both cases you know that I do not try to interpret them but to deepen their meaning, as I have done in *L'Enfant prodigue*." [22] Louis Martin-Chauffier made a similar statement in a preface to a later volume of Gide's *Oeuvres complètes*. Gide used the myths to supply "the admirably 'prepared' material they afford for commentaries or entirely personal interpretations"; they thus lose their own value and become "admirable *pretexts*." [23]

The Greek myths, then, did not present themselves to Gide as secrets in poetic form but as the distillations of a particular society to which he brought his own experience and reason. What he said about the work of art applies to his attitude towards the myths as well.

> The accomplished work of art is miraculous in that it always offers us more meaning than its author imagined; it constantly permits a richer interpretation.[24]

The applicability of this statement to the myths themselves is suggested by the context in which it is found, "Considérations sur la mythologie grecque." In this fragment, Gide insists that the Greek fables are essentially rational. They cease to teach us anything if we do not apply our reason to them, if we augment the role of Fate in the events they depict. But if we interpret them as we would interpret a consciously conceived work of art, they take on untold significance. The point is that this added meaning is bred in the eye and mind of the beholder, who brings his whole psychological and cultural orientation to bear upon the understanding of the work of art, or myth, in question. Gide affirmed this point in a letter to François Mauriac:

I maintain that the Holy Scriptures, like Greek mythology, have infinite and inexhaustible resources, and are destined to enrich themselves with each interpretation that a new spiritual orientation offers. It is in order to question them further that I do not limit myself to their first answer.[25]

But Gide not only questioned the myths, he frequently relied upon them to provide the central images of his books. The human figure as an incarnation of an attitude can define himself in reaction to his physical environment, as does Tityre in *Paludes*; but he can do as well in reaction to other figures. The need of place can thus be superseded and with it the "paysage = état d'âme" formula. With Tityre, Gide discovered the efficacy of the human figure alone as image, or more precisely, as an incarnation of a human posture. In this respect, the myths offered a multitude of such figures, which Gide later used freely in exactly this manner. As suggested by the success of Tityre, the myths and their use represent a convenient way out of his image-making dilemma and a logical outcome of his long grappling with the problem of the image.

In addition to being a vast storehouse of ready-made images, the myths offered Gide four other major advantages. First, each one was a pure and concentrated idea or attitude untainted by the bizarre, episodic, or ephemeral. Secondly, they answered his own needs for analysis by providing a means to identify and extend in fiction various aspects of his own personality. Thirdly, they represented the world of the imagination and poetry. Like André Walter, Gide profited from the poetry created by others before him. Lastly, because the mythical figures are common property, they preclude the need for elementary characterization and development, permitting Gide to begin *in medias res*. These advantages favored a basic aesthetic tenet of Gide's, litotes, which is, in essence, the device the novelist of *Paludes* described by the metaphor of the keyhole. This metaphor is particularly apt as a characterization of Gide's aesthetic because it contains two levels of significance: the keyhole represents itself as object and also what it contains upon closer scrutiny, what lies beyond it. An examination of these two levels will further clarify Gide's use of the myths as metaphoric images.

In reading and studying the myths, the gospels, or any work of art, Gide was constantly searching for the idea of the work. He was less concerned with the work of art as self-image than as likeness, in the sense given these terms by Rudolf Arnheim. A self-image, he says, is "an object that visibly expresses its own properties. Its functions derive from the properties it reveals." On the other hand, "a likeness . . . is an object treated as a statement about other objects, kinds of objects, or general properties, which are recognized in the object." [26] Gide himself has admitted this concern, suggesting it in his lecture on influence,[27] demonstrating it in much of his literary criticism, and stating it in *Propositions*:

> the work of an artist interests me fully only if I feel it exists in direct and sincere relationship with the external world and, at the same time, in intimate and secret relationship with its author.[28]

Now, in literature, what Arnheim calls the self-image is a work of art that finds its end in itself, that means only what it says, utilizing the virtues of language and of its genre for the sole purpose of communicating itself. In this class one should place the novels of Robert Louis Stevenson, *The Arabian Nights*, much of lyrical poetry, and many songs; that is to say, tales and emotions told only for the joy obtained and given in their telling. Gide applies to this class the term "sensuality." [29] In the case of pure likeness, on the other hand, the art object is but a means for contemplating or considering something beyond itself, yet with which it has important elements in common. The object itself tends to fade in the eyes of the viewer in favor of the ideal object. "The pure likeness, unrelated in space and time to its environment, requires a beholder who is able to cut his own ties in space and time." But, "the true work of art," Arnheim continues further on, "is more than a statement floating adrift." More than a pure likeness, it is also a self-image.

> It occupies, in the world of action, a place suitable to the exercise of its powers. It cannot be alone. Primitively it performs only as a thing among other things. At its most human, it rules as an embodied statement over a world in which every tool, every flower, and every rock also speaks as itself and through itself.[30]

The true work of art, then, blends to perfection both of these elements, self-image and likeness; it is a statement about the world, but inasmuch as this statement is embodied, what Gide would call "composed" or "organized," it is an object in a world of objects. The true work of art is an image of itself in time and space while at the same time it is an image alluding to something delivered of its spatial and temporal moorings, what Gide refers to as the idea. The art-object as self-image also clearly embodying an invitation to be considered as likeness, that is, as an invitation for generalization, was Gide's aesthetic ideal and his most frequently realized aesthetic tendency. It was during the composition of *Paludes* that he discovered it and during the years following that he formulated it, giving it full expression in *Littérature et morale*.

Thus, Albert Thibaudet refers to Gide as a "myth-maker" and Germaine Brée notices that "the essence of the Gidian novel . . . is its mythical character." [31] We accept the understanding of the word "myth" suggested by Thibaudet:

> Myth, introduced into art by Plato . . . is an idea carried by a narrative: an idea which is a soul, a narrative which is a body, and both of them are inseparable.[32]

But not all Gidian critics are of one mind in this matter. Jean-Michel Hennebert bluntly states,

> Gide never had the Greek sense of myth . . . but the Christian sense of parable. If his work on Greek mythology was never written, it is because the Greek fable is not essentially rational.[33]

The apparent contradiction between the two points of view as stated can be reduced to a problem of terminology. There is no doubt that Hennebert would use the term "parable" to fit the definition of "myth" offered by Thibaudet. It is interesting to note, in Hennebert's favor, that Plato's myths, which Thibaudet considers the first in literature, have been considered by others, including scholars of biblical exegesis, precisely as parable.

> The "Myths of Plato" are not myths in the strict sense of the word but are rather the parables and allegories of an acute and extraordinarily developed intellect.[34]

The two terms are close enough in meaning to cause confusion and to merit closer examination. "Myth" or "mythos" meant originally, in the critical jargon of Aristotle, "fable," "narrative," or "plot." It is easy to see how the legends received this appellation, since tragedy freely drew its plots from them. The legends originate in three basic needs of pre-scientific man, according to C. M. Bowra: "to make sense of some ritual whose significance has been forgotten, if indeed it has ever been fully understood"; "to explain natural phenomena through some dramatic, cosmological tale"; and, finally, "not to explain, but to delight." [35] Thus, the basic need that the myths satisfied was the establishment of a well-ordered universe, or, at best, well-ordered and comprehensible in terms of the real experience of the mytho-poets. Fantasy filled in where fact was lacking. Parable, on the other hand, is concerned to offer a more plausible explanation of things. [36] The parable is essentially rational. The work of one or several minds, it is a finished literary product; myth, a collective endeavor, is raw material. "Parables employ fiction, but they do it knowingly, holding it apart, in order to teach fact." [37]

Both myth and parable are particularizations of perceived or vaguely intuited abstractions. That is, both are stories, or narrative images, that function on two levels. But only for the parable was this double level a principle of composition. The parables illustrate spiritual truths in terms that were familiar to their intended listeners. As illustrations, they are plausible and realistic, thus supporting the "conviction that there is no mere analogy, but an inward affinity, between the natural order and the spiritual order." Since the parable brings its narrative into the home grounds of its audience, its realism serves to underline its problematic and argumentative nature. "The parable has the character of an argument, in that it entices the hearer to a judgment upon the situation depicted, and then challenges him, directly or by implication." [38]

This is precisely what the narrator, and Gide himself, try to do in *Paludes*; it is what characterizes so much of Gide's fiction. Many years later, in 1927, he articulated this very quality of his work:

it is not so much by offering solutions to certain problems that I can render a real service to the reader, but rather by forcing him to reflect upon those problems to which I hardly admit that he can have any other than a personal and particular solution.[39]

To say, then, that his novels are mythical in tendency would be less accurate than to affirm their parabolical nature. For although he sins against a basic tenet of the parable by dispensing with realism, he does not try to approximate truth with fictions, as do the myths; rather, he tries to create the "temptation" of a truth, that is, of an intuited idea concerning man and his condition. He becomes the articulate consciousness of this idea by creating the form by which it can be apprehended by his and future generations; moreover, he argues its plausibility by means of the parable.[40]

One might be further inclined to give credence to Hennebert's opinion for another essential reason: Gide's rigorous Protestant upbringing. Despite his own avowals,[41] his contact with the Greek world could not have been so profound as to undo the deep impression made upon him by the New Testament. His Protestant education colored not only his way of seeing reality but his way of seeing literature as well. Extremely sensitive and intelligent, he inevitably applied the rigors of biblical exegesis to all he read. The basis for such exegesis lies, of course, upon faith in the divine origin of the Scriptures. As Erich Auerbach observed, "doctrine and promise are incarnate in them and inseparable from them; for that very reason they are fraught with 'background' and mysterious, containing a second, concealed meaning." Taking the story of Isaac as an example, Auerbach continues:

Since so much in the story is dark and incomplete, and since the reader knows that God is a hidden God, his effort to interpret it constantly finds something new to feed upon.[42]

Just as Gide sought and found wisdom in the words and parables of Christ, because he believed they were the utterances of an inspired man, so, too, he sought and found wisdom in the Greek myths because he believed they were the products of a rational people. The myths were not, of course, the deliberate productions of a rational culture; they can be considered at best, if we follow Jung, as the significant workings of a collective subconscious rising up from the irrational depths of the human mind. Thus, when Gide considered the Greek myths in his essay of 1919 and postulated that they were "raisonnables," he was treating them, however inadvertently, as parables. And in reconstructing them, choosing from their numerous and frequently contradictory details only those pertinent to his idea, he recast them in parabolical form. He thus hoped to provide his reader with something constantly new to feed upon.

But Gide's long intimacy with the New Testament and its many parables permit still another view of *Paludes* and the aesthetic progress it represents. The word "parable" means "comparison" and is frequently used in the New Testament to translate the Hebrew *mashal,* itself derived from a basic verb meaning "to be like." As such, it is allied to the simile, and B. T. D. Smith attributes the origin of the parable to this rudimentary rhetorical device, seeing in the opening lines of many parables the vestiges of an original simile.[43] The biblical parable is, then, an extended metaphor that grew from a stated or implied comparison. Similarly, *Paludes* is an extended metaphor. The high metaphoric content of its central image, extended to include Tityre, the narrator and his world, suggests the common traits existing between the world of the book and the universe of the reader. One can easily imagine the narrator's gospel—and Gide's, too—in the form of a simile, after the manner of Matthew: "Your lives are like marshlands and ye know it not"; or in the form of a parable: "The Kingdom of earth shall be likened unto Tityre who made a swamp his abode. . . ."

Paludes, the first summit in Gide's literary career, expresses and implies with most consummate artistry the Gidian aesthetic and the form most of his fictional works take. This form is the parable, the natural and logical outcome of his long groping with the problem of that expressive aesthetic unit, the image.

VII

Conclusion: The A Priori Novel

Gide's rehandling of the classical legends has earned him a reputation as one of the leaders of the recent myth-making vogue, even though less than half of his fictional and dramatic works can be properly classified as mythical. Except for occasional returns, when inspiration was flagging during his later years, he abandoned the myths as he reached the peak of his literary output. But it was essentially through them that he developed an aesthetic outlook that enabled him to transcend them and to apply his new techniques to nonmythical material.

The figure of Narcisse, which predates Gide's discoveries of late 1894, has comparatively little value as a pure image. A symbol for introspection, the figure is handled as a "likeness" having no other function than that of a concrete sign for an abstract idea. The later Gidian myths, too, are "likenesses"; they are pictures—perhaps, more justly, moving-pictures—of a general human truth Gide has perceived in the raw mythic material at his disposal. But this is as far as the comparison can go. The later myths are not, properly speaking, symbols but rather extended metaphors. Direct linking of the idea with its vehicle occurs only at the beginning of the work of art, or at the time of its "imagination." Thereafter, it is not the idea that controls the development of the work, as in *Le Traité*, but rather its image. Each myth is developed to its limit on its own terms and never on those that gave rise to both elements of the initial comparison. Since the myths are rational, as Gide claimed, they can be exploited and handled as "self-images" or particularizations. Like the details of a biblical parable, their elements are dependent only upon the initial image; they thus fit in perfectly and do not strain credulity. In *Paludes*, for example, Gide implies that "we are like Tityre who made a swamp his home." As in a biblical parable, the point of comparison is at the beginning; all else in *Paludes* develops only according to the latter part of the comparison: "Tityre made a swamp his home." Yet the initial comparison, if not constantly referred to in the course of the narrative, permeates the atmosphere of the book. Because of this persistence, explicit or implicit, the Gidian parable, like its biblical models, is fraught with background. A deeper level of meaning suggested in Gide's simple narratives makes "likenesses" of what he apparently treats only as "self-images."

Gide did not deny the presence of a deeper level of meaning in his works but he repeatedly admonished his reader to take them primarily as works of art and not as expositions of ideas; he urged that we consider them, at most, as an invitation to generalize. Now if we go against his wishes for a moment and consider his myths only as "likenesses," we shall see how they approach the parable in still another way. His myths, it was said earlier, are developed on their own terms and not on those of the idea alone. But from another point of view, the idea itself, in its concrete and usually human form, is brought to its limit, that is, to its logical conclusion. In his myths Gide traces the birth of an idea, its growth and struggle for survival, its ultimate defeat or victory. An idea can be defeated when it fails to isolate itself and dominate its host. In such a case the human personality resists its control and integrates it with other ideas, thus establishing a healthy balance. Such happy endings are rare in Gidian fiction, occurring only in *Philoctète*, where self-abnegation does not lead to disaster as in *La Porte étroite*, simply because the hero remains free and controls his behavior—he remains independent of the idea to which he accedes; in *Thésée*, in which the hero toys with several ideas but always returns to the major path of his life, guided by the thread of his past; and, in part, in *Le Prométhée mal enchaîné*, in which, we shall see, the protagonist is finally persuaded to shed a dominating idea. But, on the other hand, the victorious idea comes to an ironic end: it destroys not only its host but itself as well. This is more frequently the case among Gide's myths, notably *Saül*, *Le Roi Candaule*, *Bethsabé*, *Oedipe*, and especially Coclès and Damoclès of *Le Prométhée*. "Le Retour de l'enfant prodigue" (Gide's only biblical parable), belongs to this class, although, strictly speaking, the idea is not victorious. Obsessed, like the author of *Paludes*, by the desire to go beyond himself and to discover who he is, the prodigal son cannot sustain the hardships of freedom and finds himself without moral as well as material resources. He returns to the fold, refusing—even unable—to risk being dominated by the idea of personal freedom. The idea, then, fails for him, but it has caused his failure to become an individual. Forced to accept an externally imposed identity, he ends tragically, in a moral sense, as do Saül and Candaule.

Whether or not the idea is victorious, it is clear that Gide's myths concentrate upon the career a given idea will have in rather rigorously defined circumstances. These circumstances are, to be sure, entirely governed by the central metaphoric image of a given work, by the "imagined" form the idea has taken. Here we come to the center of the parabolical construction of Gide's myths. Why, one may ask with Angèle, must Tityre be unable to catch fish? Why, in other words, must an idea succeed or fail in a given situation? Angèle's literary friend answers on aesthetic grounds, stating that he is more concerned with truth than realism and that, in the case of Tityre, it is a question of psychological truth. Angèle is not entirely satisfied with this answer. Her standards of judgment are based on reality, and, however strange it may seem, Tityre has become real for her. She sees him as a living being and brings her whole background to bear upon understanding him. The narrator has prodded Angèle, perhaps without entirely realizing it, into some sort of self-identification with his hero.[1]

To elicit such identification is, in part, the reason for realism in the biblical parables. In addition to suggesting a natural affinity between the natural order and the spiritual order of the universe, realism in the parables arises out of their fundamental purpose: to teach. The parables are drawn from life in order to attract the listener's attention, prodding him into identification with the matter at hand, arresting him "by [their] vividness or strangeness and leaving the mind in sufficient doubt about [their] precise application to tease it to active thought."[2] Herein lies the argumentative nature of the parables. Gide's mythical parables differ from biblical parables for the most part in that they dispense with realism. Their very strangeness teases the reader's mind to active thought.

In *Paludes*, Gide wanted to be sure that his reader would think about stagnancy in the human personality, and so he reinforced the structure of his parable with the "en abyme" construction. Existing at first only in Tityre, the idea of immobility extends itself to Richard, to the narrator, to their whole society, and ultimately to the reader and his world. Gide first elicits the reader's sympathy and collaboration, prods him to make a judgment upon the characters, and finally forces him to apply this judgment to himself, to reflect on these very problems, and to justify his identification.

Le Prométhée mal enchaîné is probably the clearest illustration of Gide's argumentation by myth. Much, perhaps too much, has been made of the gratuitous act that Gide first developed here and not enough of its illustrations. But it is precisely in its illustrative episodes that the theory is put to the test, in the persons of two unsuspecting and undistinguished humans, Coclès and Damoclès. One day, out of the blue, an unknown gentleman delivers to Coclès an undeserved slap in the face and to Damoclès an unearned five-hundred-franc bill. Damoclès ultimately dies because he cannot determine the reason for his sudden gift. Coclès, victimized without reason by the same event, suddenly thrives in a society easily enflamed against injustice. Both lives are profoundly modified by the gratuitous event that has befallen them, that has selected them from the throng, and has given them an identity. And each remains faithful to his newly acquired identity. Damoclès broods over his gift until he succumbs to brain fever brought on by his obsession. Coclès, faring well as a result of his slap and lost eye, seeks to be unjustly victimized again. Each, like the legendary Prometheus, is thus chained to an eagle. In Gide's version, Prométhée even posits the necessity of everyone's possessing one. Prométhée indeed has his own, which he wears on his shoulders. But Damoclès' example convinces Prométhée that such devotion may endanger one's freedom to test other ideas in the future. He thereupon roasts his eagle and writes a book with one of its feathers. He thus discards his original principle that everyone must devote himself to the full development of an idea through one's own person. He is "mal enchaîné" because he is able to shed what was for him an identity and to search for a new one.

Here the argumentative nature of the book becomes apparent. For Prométhée, the line of reasoning that everyone must have an eagle has, in reality, the status of hypothesis. It is Damoclès and Coclès who test this hypothesis from different points of view. Damoclès represents its full development; he tests its validity by totally committing himself to it and, unlike Coclès, by living it through to the end. Neither one can go beyond Cartesian cause and effect, but, where Damoclès emphasizes the cause of the event, Coclès concerns himself with repeating its effect; he observes about himself and Damoclès that "we have never been able to understand each other; our points of view are diametrically opposed." [3] He looks to the future in the hope that a similar event, a new slap, will result in the same good fortune as the first. Although Coclès and Damoclès are equally impressed by Prométhée's first speech and are equally devoted to their eagle, only Damoclès brings his to its logical conclusion. Gide gives a hint, however, that Coclès is in danger of a similar end. After Prométhée's final fable, Coclès fails to see its relevancy to Damoclès' death. "Had there been more of it you wouldn't have laughed so much," [4] Prométhée answers. The point of this response seems clear: had the message been transparent Coclès would have understood Prométhée's complete reversal of position, his implied advice to kill his eagle and discard the identity he so cherishes. This realization dawns upon Coclès a few moments later when he understands that Prométhée has indeed killed his own eagle. Thus Coclès, like Damoclès, tests an idea, but in his case the test is incomplete; he still has time to profit from Damoclès' failure, as does, in fact, Prométhée.

In *Philoctète*, the argumentative nature of Gide's parables becomes obvious in the confrontation of two diametrically opposed views on duty and virtue. The conflict between Ulysse and Philoctète is one that had tormented Gide as early as 1890,[5] the difference between being and appearing. Both argue the validity of their respective positions before Néoptolème, who, as a proxy for the reader, oscillates between them. He finally understands and accepts Philoctète's point of view, thereby underlining the victory over the traditional concept of duty to external institutions. The virtue Philoctète enacts is one of self-abnegation for a fuller and more authentic expression of himself. Alone on his island, he expresses himself in total freedom and without the inhibiting presence of an audience. Yet so long as he possesses the bow and arrows of Hercules—the weapons needed to vanquish the Trojans—he exists in the minds of his countrymen and is, in this way, still tied to them. By relinquishing his weapons he severs all connections with the Greeks and with his own identity as a Greek. Completely isolated, he is completely free to be; he is no longer a Greek but just a human being, free to create a non-ethnic identity for himself. Thus Philoctète not only argues in favor of his virtue but, by putting it into action, demonstrates its validity. "They will not return," he says after Ulysse and his charge have left; "they no longer have any bow to get . . . I am happy." [6]

Gide's attainment at La Brévine was not limited to an adept use of the myths; it was most importantly the discovery of the narrative tool he derived from manipulating them. He soon realized that if the exposition of an idea, developed and tested in the purely artificial form of a myth, as in *Paludes* or *Le Prométhée*, is feasible as a novel, so too is the same process in modern dress, in an equally artificial yet contemporary analogue of the myths. If Tityre can be considered as an image of an idea so placed in a particular landscape as to develop to its logical limits, a contemporary image following the same development can be as cogent and fictionally effective. A lethargic novelist might be made to function plausibly in a fictional landscape without the inlaid figure of Tityre. Saül modernized does, in effect, become Michel of *L'Immoraliste*.

Once again Gide suggests this development during his Neuchâtel sojourn. In an unpublished page of the journal, under the dateline of late October, 1894, he made the following remarks concerning the novel:

Conclusion: *The A Priori Novel*

Le roman doit prouver à présent qu'il peut être autre chose qu'un miroir promené le long du chemin—qu'il peut être supérieur et *a priori*—c'est-à-dire déduit, c'est-à-dire *composé*, c'est-à-dire oeuvre d'art.[7]

Further on in the same entry, he develops more fully these brief notations:

Nous sommes a prioristes enragés. J'ai bon espoir que le roman le prouvera. . . . Le roman prouvera qu'il peut peindre autre chose que la réalité—directement l'émotion et la pensée; il montrera jusqu'à quel point il peut être déduit, *avant l'expérience des choses*—jusqu'à quel point c'est-à-dire il peut être composé—c'est-à-dire oeuvre d'art. Il montrera qu'il peut être oeuvre d'art, composé de toutes pièces, d'un réalisme non des petits faits et contingents, mais supérieur—de l'idéorealisme comme disait Mauclair [8]—qu'il soit plus réel, plus vrai que les choses de la soi-disant réalité, comme le triangle mathématique est plus réel et plus vrai que les triangles imparfaits des arpenteurs. Il faut que dans leur rapport même chaque partie d'une oeuvre prouve la vérité de chaque autre—il n'est pas besoin d'autre preuve. Rien d'irritant comme le témoignage que Monsieur de Gourmont donne à tout ce qu'il avance—il a vu! il a entendu! comme si la preuve par le réel était nécessaire. Comme si le monde de l'esprit différait en rien du monde des choses et que le microcosme fût régi par d'autres lois que le macrocosme. L'un est sûr, l'autre est incertain . . . c'est toute la différence.[9]

I quote the long text reproduced by Jean Delay because it contains the only remarks that represent in any way the consciousness of a breakthrough in Gide's development during the period at La Brévine. Delay sees the importance of this text in that it applies the precepts of *Le Traité du Narcisse* to the art of the novel. Yet one might be at a loss to see exactly which precepts of *Le Traité* reappear here. Gide, or the Poet, in that work, is seeking the true reality hidden by the exterior world. The Poet, we recall, contemplates the imperfect forms of reality in order to seize the Idea and clothe it in a purely expressive symbol. If anything, he is an "a postérioriste enragé." The Poet, therefore, operates on another theory than the one Gide expounded in 1894—that the novelist is "a prioriste" and that the novel can be composed before the experience of things. It is true that the net result of both theories is more or less the same: both seek what can be described as "idéoréalisme." But this term can be understood in at least two ways, each depending upon a different understanding of the word "idée." We are again obliged to distinguish between the Platonic Idea, or archetype, and the Leibnizian Idea, or potential truth. In *Le Traité* Gide sought the superior reality of archetypes, while later he concerned himself with the superior reality of thought and feeling arising from action yet to occur.

What is significant in the 1894 journal entry quoted above is the statement on method: "Il faut que dans leur rapport même chaque partie d'une oeuvre prouve la vérité de chaque autre." This remark aptly applies to Gide's development at the time and subsequently, yet it recalls, not *Le Traité*, but *Les Cahiers*, as, for example, the discussion of Walter's novel at the opening of the second *cahier*:

Spinoza's arrangement for his Ethics—transpose it to the novel! Geometric lines. A novel is a theorem.[10]

Earlier in this same section, he refers to the novel as a demonstration. Thus the method Gide used in nearly all his imaginative works seems to have been present—in theory if not in practice—as early as 1891.[11]

If the method changed little, the subject matter changed considerably. From archetype, the meaning of Idea shaded into potential truth, or untested and unlived thought. Imagined and composed in a work of art, the idea argues its feasibility by the geometrical and logical development of the "récit." For the "récit" is the analogue in modern dress of Gide's mythic parables. It follows in structure and development the myths Gide reworked in his early and late periods.

Gide suggests the genesis of several of his "récits" in the *Journal*, suggestions which clearly demonstrate their kinship to mythic parables. Prefigurations or "symboles de l'oeuvre" exist in the early journals for both *L'Immoraliste* and *La Porte étroite*; both resemble in form and tone the first notation of *Paludes*. In an earlier discussion these prefigurations were considered the first imagined form of the idea Gide was to develop in his work. But they contain as well a hint of the work's plot and ultimate denouement, that is, they express a dynamic relationship, or the arrangement of human elements in a scenario form. The first form of *Paludes* was *Angèle ou le pauvre petit voyage*: "Elle avait peur de la volupté comme une chose trop forte et qui l'aurait pu tuer." In the process of composing *Paludes* Gide broadened the fear of "volupté" to encompass the fear of all and any sort of movement or activity. The book is especially interesting in this light because it contains within the same structure two "imaged" forms of the idea rendered with varying degrees of reality. On the level of each form the idea is played out by the human figures of Tityre and the narrator. Each figure develops to the most extreme position plausible on its own level. Because the narrator is more credible as a human being living in our own reality than the remote and intense classical figure of Tityre, he more readily imposes his presence upon us. The "récits" limit themselves to our reality, to the higher level of plausibility suggested by the narrator in *Paludes*. The Gidian parable, by dispensing with anachronism, comes to satisfy, in the "récits," the thus-far neglected imperative of the biblical form: realism. Alissa and Jérôme, Michel, the pastor of *La Symphonie pastorale*, Lacase, the three protagonists of the trilogy, *L'Ecole des femmes*, are all potential participants in our reality: they could have existed as they are in our world. Yet all are as much incarnations of an idea as are Tityre and his biographer, as Prométhée, Saül, and Candaule.[12]

Although the "récits" are so constructed that their idea is easily perceivable, Gide himself made several statements at various times in his career that leave no doubt in our mind as to these ideas. Thus one can safely affirm that Michel represents "precipitate sensuality," Alissa, the reverse side of the coin, or "frantic spirituality"; *La Symphonie pastorale* demonstrates a form of self-deception, *Isabelle*, a form of "Romantic imagination," and finally *Les Faux-Monnayeurs*, a multiple and simultaneous exposition of various modes of deception and falsification.[13]

The exposition, or rather, the geometric demonstration of the incarnated idea entails a unilinear development; each new event or fact is prepared by those preceding it, and it, in turn, lays the groundwork for what is to follow. Since the idea takes on human form, the demonstration amounts to a rigorous psychological proof. The essence of this proof lies in what Gide called the composition of a work, which we have dubbed the work's scenario. The first prefiguration of *L'Immoraliste* most clearly fits this description, as we have seen.

Sa précipitation était telle qu'il s'écorchait les mains aux serrures.

The statement is pithy; it poses questions such as, where was he enclosed and why, what must be the nature of such an enclosure to lead him to rush headlong and carelessly out of it? Many more subtle questions of a psychological nature immediately come to mind: was he aware of the danger and, if so, how did he explain it; was his behavior impulsive or reasoned?

Suggested answers to these questions and many others are demonstrated in the person of Michel. But Gide does not analyze Michel; the analysis is present in the demonstration itself. Gide exhibits the path traced by Michel from rigid asceticism to nearly total hedonism. In keeping with the spirit of demonstration, Gide employs the first person narrative: Michel, well within the confines of subjectivity, relates the events of his life simply, without modesty or pride, more simply than if he were speaking to himself.[14] He makes no effort to condemn or condone, but only recounts the events that led him to the impasse in which he finds himself. He seeks to understand and to explain to his listeners (and readers) the path he took. With such liberty given his protagonist, Gide hoped to have him hang himself, with, of course, the complicity of the reader. But because the development and sequence of events are so logical and because the final result is so patently immoral (Gide himself helps us to this conclusion by the book's title), the reader is at pains to determine exactly where Michel went wrong. Thus, as Michel challenges his listeners, Gide challenges his readers. "Michel remained silent for a long time," observes the reader's proxy in one of his rare intrusions in the narrative.

> We also kept quiet, each of us seized by a strange uneasiness. It seemed to us, alas, that by recounting his action, he had made it more legitimate. By not knowing where to disapprove, in the slow explanation he gave of it, we

almost became accomplices. It was as if we were involved in it.[15]

The same procedure is implicit, if not explicit as in *L'Immoraliste*, in the other "récits." In *La Symphonie pastorale*, it is the pastor's renegade son who challenges the reader to judge his father's behavior. In an effort to justify his conversion to Catholicism, Jacques is reluctant to accuse his father, he says, but he does not refuse to implicate him in his conversion: "it's the example of your error that has guided me," [16] he finally tells him. Here again a secondary character gives expression to the key aspect of the Gidian parable: the "récits" are examples of what not to do. It was no doubt with this in mind that Gide described his books as ironical and critical.[17]

The demonstration of *La Porte étroite* is a trifle more complex in that it is double. Two developments are set side by side; each is represented by the narrators, Alissa and Jérôme. Jérôme's demonstration is entirely dependent, however, upon Alissa's. She is truly the sole protagonist of the novel; it is her striving that is symbolized by the title and that controls the unfolding of the narrative. She is the example of a mystic tendency, of self-abnegation brought to its logical conclusion in death. Her mode of worship is self-destructive because it is never satisfied. Since God does not respond to her, she feels she has not wisely or sufficiently adored. She is caught in this cycle and yet has sacrificed too much to yield to the temptation of blasphemy. The last entry in her journal ironically synthesizes this impasse: "I would like to die, now, quickly, before I understand once more that I am alone." [18] But she is no more alone than Jérôme, who after ten years is still unable to go beyond his love for her.[19] He, in turn, illustrates by his canine fidelity the possible side-effects of Alissa's excluding piety. Thus her obsession only succeeds in destroying the lives of two people who might otherwise have lived happily and fruitfully together.

The futility of their lives, of Alissa's gesture, is suggested by the silence and banality of the novel's last line: "A servant entered, bringing the lamp." [20] The intensity of love, of mysticism, of self-sacrifice, in a word, of superhuman feelings, ends in an emptiness so total that so banal an observation as this can fill it. This end, "stupid as life," [21] Flaubert would no doubt have said about it, puts into question Alissa's piety and indeed any extreme and self-denying mysticism. The import of the novel thus transcends its final pages and enters into the world of the careful reader. His complicity is inescapable.

To go beyond the monolithic structure of the "récit" and to compose a novel as complex and unresolved as life itself was a temptation Gide was happily unable to resist. Yet in *Les Faux-Monnayeurs*, Gide interspersed a number of such "récits." These monographs [22] revolve, however, about a single theme—falseness—symbolized in the novel's title. Upon closer consideration of Gide's early work, one form of this theme, self-deception, can be seen as basic to all of his "récits"; but only as he produced them did he apparently come to realize that it lay at the core of his socio-moral criticism. He gave the label "une forme de mensonge à soi-même," a form of self-deception, only to *La Symphonie pastorale*, the last of the great "récits," but the earlier ones, although not so labeled, clearly fit the same description. Michel as well as Alissa, Gérard Lacase, Eveline, Robert, and Geneviève, all illustrate various forms of self-deception. For, in most cases, the Gidian protagonist limits himself and his development to an a priori notion of what he himself is. Since this notion frequently springs from the picture others have of him, he finds himself living up to ideals they have formulated for him, which have no real support in himself. He thus neglects his authentic personality, that is, the personality he could have become in freer circumstances, and he becomes, instead, a counterfeit being.

In *Les Faux-Monnayeurs*, many such counterfeit personalities appear, and it is not difficult to find here analogues of the earlier protagonists. To be sure, Gide refused to cover terrain already treated in earlier "récits," and thus the full demonstration of several forms of self-deception is not undertaken in the novel. Yet such figures do appear, if only cursorily. Vincent Molinier or Sarah Vedel suggests the evolution of Michel; Boris, that of Alissa; the Vedels, grandfather and father, suggest shadings of the pastor in *La Symphonie pastorale*; one might even be tempted to see the would-be-novelist of *Isabelle* in Robert de Passavant or, more feasibly, and on a grander scale, in Edouard. Most of the characters in *Les Faux-Monnayeurs* represent new types and forms of self-deception. In each there is implicit or explicit the subject matter of a complete "récit," the demonstration of a form of behavior based on an idea. The "pères de famille," Molinier and Profitendieu, both enamoured of their station in life, become parodies à la Daumier of Justice Department officials; Sophroniska remains faithful to her conception of a practicing Freudian; Passavant, convinced of his genius, permits himself all sorts of transgressions, etc. But not all the novel's characters are finished counterfeit products. Several are in the process of becoming so: Sarah and Armand Vedel, Vincent Molinier (whose complete curve is barely traced in the novel). Others, including the principal characters, make an initial false step but, by force of intelligence and will, break the hold of self-deception and avoid fabricated personalities; Laura, Bernard, and Olivier are among those few who manage to escape the counterfeit, after having made false starts.

What these characters have in common, at least from the point of view of the novelist, what makes of their lives the possible subject matter of an independent Gidian "récit," is the demonstration of a purely personal problem: coming to terms with oneself. Very rarely in the history of occidental literature, Gide observed in the Dostoievsky lectures, has the novel been concerned with man's relationship with himself, or with God.[23] The study of these relationships has been Gide's prime concern since *Les Cahiers d'André Walter* and understandably forms the major concern of *Les Faux-Monnayeurs*. Like the earlier works, this is a critical book. But *Les Faux-Monnayeurs* is complicated by the fusion of a number of simultaneous demonstrations; each offers a slightly different approach to the main problem, which is symbolized by the title of the book and its central episode, the passing of counterfeit coins. This image, like the swamp in *Paludes*, infects all the apparently disparate elements of the book; the counterfeit coins are the standard by which are measured the things and beings of his fictional world. But because the book is composed of various parabolical narratives which challenge the reader, these coins may be said to represent the same standard for things and beings in his world.

With *Les Faux-Monnayeurs* Gide created his first and only universal demonstration of various solutions to an essential problem in the human personality. For all its complexity, baroque or cubist,[24] Gide's only novel is in essence made up of many interwoven parables. This basic narrative unit arose from his use and misuse of yet another more basic literary unit, the image as metaphoric vehicle for an abstract idea. It is thus fitting that the title and organizing principle of his first novel should be such an image.

Of all the French writers of the first half of the twentieth century, Gide offers by far the greatest resistance to codification, to labels of any kind, to the one-word or one-phrase descriptions that fill manuals of literature. Moreover, in the

unfolding of his life and the development of his philosophy—
if one may use so ponderous a term—and his aesthetic, there
appears no decisive influence or sharp turning point, no
moment of which one can truly say that here Gide suddenly
became all he was to express subsequently. Even the much-
celebrated journey to North Africa and his resulting sensual
renascence were prepared well in advance, as Jean Delay has
so ably shown. In the more limited and critically controllable
area of aesthetics, one recognizes something of a turning point
in *Paludes*. But even here, discoveries in aesthetics prove to
be basically refinements of principles already present, if only
in rough form, in the earlier works. From *Les Cahiers d'André
Walter* to *Paludes*, his first complete artistic success and truly
a breviary of the Gidian aesthetic, Gide worked out the
aesthetic principles that were to guide him to and through
the most productive periods of his life. Like Ariadne's thread,
these principles were the guides that enabled him to handle
material of great variety.

Clarifying these principles helps us to a more profound
understanding of Gide's later masterpieces and also may
indicate some of the tendencies of the modern novel. The
modern parable, using mythic or modern material, can be
found in many works by Gide's younger colleagues; one need
mention only Anouilh, Giraudoux, Sartre, Cocteau, and even
Montherlant, who joins the group with his fragment *Pasiphaë*
and his version of the Don Juan legend. But closest to Gide in
spiritual and aesthetic outlook is Albert Camus. His *Mythe de
Sisyphe* comes immediately to mind, but most like the Gidian
parables are *L'Etranger* and *La Chute*; the last, a unilinear
demonstration which has been called a tour de force, is
basically similar to *L'Immoraliste*. One might even be tempted
to extend Gide's influence to the new novel's experimentation
in fusing the personal essay and the novel. But however far

one might be willing to go in the search for outgrowths of Gide's aesthetic principles, one must inevitably acknowledge that these principles are, in the last analysis, products of their unique creator. They are personal solutions to personal subjective problems.

Notes

The sources of the material quoted in the Preface are:

André Gide, "Journal," Carnet 3 (unpublished page, May, 1889) in the Bibliothèque littéraire Jacques Doucet;
André Gide, "*Les Nourritures terrestres,* préface de l'édition de 1927," *Oeuvres complètes,* II, 229. References to this edition are hereafter abbreviated, *OC.*

INTRODUCTION

1. André Gide, *Si le Grain ne meurt* (1926), in *Journal, 1939–1949, Souvenirs,* Bibliothèque de la Pléiade (Paris: Gallimard, 1954), p. 362. References to the *Journal, 1889–1949,* to *Si le Grain ne meurt,* and other memoirs, will be found in the two Pléiade volumes, hereafter abbreviated, *JAG.*
2. *JAG,* I, 770. Entry dated October 10, 1923.
3. "Projet de conférence pour Berlin (1928)," *Feuillets, OC,* XV, 513.
4. *Ainsi soit-il ou Les Jeux sont faits* (1952), *JAG,* II, 1226f.
5. See journal entry dated December 20, 1924, *JAG,* I, 798ff., and *Ainsi soit-il,* in *JAG,* II, 1200ff.
6. The lectures were delivered at the Collège de France from December 1, 1927, to March 8, 1928.
7. Pierre Janet, *L'Evolution de la mémoire et de la notion du temps* (Paris: A. Cahine, 1928), p. 310ff.
8. *Ibid.,* pp. 311f., 353.
9. *Ibid.,* pp. 431f.
10. *Ainsi soit-il, JAG,* II, 1227.
11. Jean Delay, *La Jeunesse d'André Gide* (Paris: Gallimard, 1956–57), I, 242.

Notes (Chapter I)

12. *Ibid.*, I, 584. See Sigmund Freud, "Formulations regarding the two Principles in Mental Functioning," *Collected Papers* (London: Hogarth, 1948), IV, 19.
13. *Ainsi soit-il, JAG,* II, 1227.
14. *Si le Grain ne meurt, JAG,* II, 361.
15. *Ibid., JAG,* II, 362.
16. *Ibid.*
17. *JAG,* I, 929. Entry dated July 28, 1929.
18. Both Zola and Maupassant admitted to this "illusion." See Zola, "Lettre à Antony Valabrègue" (1864), *Les Oeuvres complètes d'Emile Zola,* éd. Maurice Le Blond (Paris: Imp. Bernouard, 1927–29), XLVIII, 250, 255f., and Maupassant, "Préface à *Pierre et Jean,*" *Les Oeuvres complètes de Guy de Maupassant* (Paris: Conard, 1908–28), XII, xi, xv.
19. C. Day Lewis, *The Poetic Image* (London: Jonathan Cape, 1947), pp. 19, 22.
20. *Les Faux-Monnayeurs, OC,* XII, 271.

CHAPTER I

1. Entry dated September 14, 1891, "Cahier de notes de lectures" in the Bibliothèque Littéraire Jacques Doucet. "This I believe will have been my greatest influence."
2. Arthur Schopenhauer, *The World as Will and Idea,* trans. R. B. Haldane and J. Kemp (London: Kegan Paul, 1907), I, 302f. Gide probably read A. Burdeau's translation, *Le Monde comme volonté et représentation,* 2 vols. (Paris: Félix Alcan, 1888–89). Cf. *Si le Grain ne meurt, JAG,* II, 519.
3. *Si le Grain ne meurt, JAG,* I, 313f.
4. *Ibid.*, I, 314.
5. "Journal," Carnet 3 (unpublished page, March, 1887). [One must paint landscape and phenomena only in their relationship to the soul.] For a similar remark see Stéphane Mallarmé, *Oeuvres complètes,* Bibliothèque de la Pléiade (Paris: Gallimard, 1945), p. 869. Gide also says here: "Il faut aussi renoncer à peindre tout ce qui n'est pas du sentiment. . . . Rien de fatigant, d'ennuyeux comme les descriptions de Gautier lorsqu'aucune émotion ne les féconde." [One must also forego painting anything that is not related to feeling. . . . There is nothing so tiring, so boring, as Gautier's descriptions when no emotion fecundates them.]

Notes (Chapter I)

6. *Si le Grain ne meurt*, *JAG*, II, 489.
7. *Ibid.*, *JAG*, II, 505.
8. "Journal," Carnet 3 (unpublished page, August, 1888). [With verse, one is too much a slave.]
9. *Si le Grain ne meurt*, *JAG*, II, 506. In the early journal, Gide calls these his first serious verses ("Journal," Carnet 3, May 17, 1888). [I wanted to speak to him; he did not understand me./When I said I was in love, he began to smile./I should have found better words to tell him,/Have feigned some scorn about my secret love,/Appeared unmoved, perhaps even laughed about it.]
10. *Si le Grain ne meurt*, *JAG*, II, 506. The incident probably took place in May, 1888. See Delay, I, 389.
11. He settled himself in a chalet at Menthon on the shores of Lake Annecy in the Dauphiné. He left Paris May 27, 1890, and returned July 3, 1890, without having completed his book however. Not until October 19 of that year did he have the manuscript ready for publication. See Delay, I, 446, 470.
12. *Si le Grain ne meurt*, *JAG*, II, 521. [In the spring I felt the moment had come, but in order to write my book, I had to have solitude. . . . In the complete solitude in which I lived, I was able to work myself up to a white-hot fervor and to maintain myself in that state of lyrical ecstasy, outside of which I thought it improper to write.]
13. See *Et nunc manet in te*, *JAG*, II, 1123f.
14. *Les Cahiers d'André Walter*, *OC*, I, 175.
15. *Ibid.*, *OC*, I, 95. [One character alone, even someone commonplace, or rather his mind, is the sole common ground where the drama unfolds, the closed field where the adversaries enter into combat.]
16. *Ibid.*, *OC*, I, 97. [For the angel, the ever greater desire to ascend; he needs a goal and must aspire to it: it is towards you, Emmanuèle, ideally superior. (And here, the whole impossible novel.)]
17. *Si le Grain ne meurt*, *JAG*, II, 522. See also *JAG*, I, 795 (November 21, 1924), and the preface to the 1930 edition of *Les Cahiers*, *OC*, I, 201–03.
18. Jean Hytier, *André Gide*, tr. Richard Howard (Garden City, N.Y.: Doubleday, 1962), p. 27. In the light of Hytier's *Le Plaisir poétique* (Paris: Presses universitaires de France, 1923), p. 112, and *Les Arts de la littérature* (Alger: Charlot, 1945), pp. 26f., we

understand theme to mean a particular poetic sentiment or truth represented or evoked by means of pretexts, that is, particular and concrete details.

19. Gide had been familiar with the *Journal intime* of Henri-Frédéric Amiel since 1885 and had read the *Journal* of Marie Bashkirtseff during the months of July and August, 1890. See Delay, I, 468.
20. *OC*, I, 3f.
21. *Notes d'un voyage en Bretagne*, *OC*, I, 9. The notes were written during his trip through Brittany in the summer of 1889. He was undecided about the spelling of his hero's name but finally chose Allain. [While returning, I felt the strange uneasiness which precedes creation; I saw once again, as happened occasionally before, bits of the story of *Alain* or of the *Education*, which suddenly became clear as daylight.]
22. Delay, I, 412.
23. Percy Lubbock, *The Craft of Fiction* (New York: Viking, 1957), p. 251. This study, based upon the novels and critical writing of Henry James, was first published in 1921.
24. *Les Faux-Monnayeurs*, *OC*, XII, 274. [If I do not succeed in writing this book, it will be because the history of the book will have interested me more than the book itself; it will have taken its place; and it will be just as well.]
25. *Si le Grain ne meurt*, *JAG*, II, 506. [The preoccupation I lived in had the serious inconvenience of turning all my attentive faculties towards introspection. I wrote and wanted to write only what was intimate.]
26. *Littérature et morale*, *JAG*, I, 90.
27. *Si le Grain ne meurt*, *JAG*, II, 522.
28. For a résumé of the critical reception of *Les Cahiers*, see Justin O'Brien, *Portrait of André Gide, A Critical Biography* (New York: Alfred A. Knopf, 1953), pp. 58ff., and Delay, I, 488ff. See also the 1930 edition of *Les Cahiers* (Paris: Les Oeuvres représentatives, 1930).
29. Letter to André Gide, January 20, 1891. In Delay, I, 488.
30. Letter to André Gide, May 9, 1891. In Delay, I, 490.
31. See Delay, I, 491.
32. In Delay, I, 468. [It is evident that one can never succeed in making others feel one's own emotion in its intensity, that it is better to resign oneself immediately and, with talent, insinuate emotion—make it felt symbolically, suggestively.]

33. Prior to this first recalled incident, and very early in the book there is, it is true, the clearly delineated scene of Mme Walter's death. This scene, however, does little more than set the stage for all that follows. It is on her deathbed that Mme Walter makes her son promise to give up Emmanuèle, and there too, that she subsequently celebrates Emmanuèle's engagement to T. See *OC*, I, 29f.
34. This and the following quotations are from *Les Cahiers*, *OC*, I, 32–39. [The education of a soul; to form it in one's own way—a soul, loving and loved, so resembling one's own that the two understand each other, and from so far away that nothing can separate them. . . . We learned everything together; I imagined only those joys I shared with you (*OC*, I, 32). To suffer together, together to become impassioned (*OC*, I, 34). The great tremor both moral and physical, that stirs you before sublime things and that we each thought we had experienced alone, that we did not speak of it to one another—what joy when we discovered it was the same in each: it was a great feeling (*OC*, I, 36). And, as it was getting late, we fell asleep, dreaming, one pressed against the other, our hands joined (*OC*, I, 38).]
35. *Ibid.*, *OC*, I, 86.
36. *Ibid.*, *OC*, I, 52f.
37. *Ibid.*, *OC*, I, 63.
38. *Ibid.*, *OC*, I, 98.
39. *Ibid.*, *OC*, I, 143.
40. *Ibid.*, *OC*, I, 173.
41. Hytier, *André Gide*, p. 27.
42. *Les Cahiers*, *OC*, I, 53.
43. *Ibid.*, *OC*, I, 63.
44. In Paul Iseler, *Les Débuts d'André Gide vus par Pierre Louÿs* (Paris: Editions du Sagittaire, 1937), p. 95. The letter is dated June 30, 1890.

CHAPTER II

1. Preface to the 1930 edition of *Les Cahiers d'André Walter*, *OC*, I, 202f.
2. *Caractères*, *OC*, XII, 9.
3. H. W. Fowler, "Simile and Metaphor," *A Dictionary of Modern English Usage*, 2nd. ed. (New York: Oxford University Press, 1965).

4. William Butler Yeats, *Essays and Introductions* (New York: Macmillan, 1961), p. 116.

5. Works such as *Treasure Island* or *The Arabian Nights,* for example, are characterized by the absence of thought, Gide suggests in several letters to Angèle (*OC,* III, 189, 221). In this connection he defines sensuality in literature as the consideration of the present moment, and the present object as an end, not as a means (*OC,* III, 220).

6. Schopenhauer, *The World as Will and Idea,* I, 317, 322.

7. Although the poetic device he names is "epithet," it is clear that he means "image," that linguistic unit "by means of which the universality of every concept is narrowed more and more till we reach the perceptible" (Schopenhauer, I, 314). He is, however, somewhat limited in his notions of symbol; he feels that the symbol, taken in its narrowest meaning, is based on agreement and once this is forgotten the symbol is mute. See I, 308ff.

8. *Les Cahiers d'André Walter, OC,* I, 127.

9. Schopenhauer, I, 322.

10. *Les Cahiers, OC,* I, 130.

11. *Ibid., OC,* I, 96.

12. *Ibid., OC,* I, 136. [I was playing, and the overworked piano was trembling in all its strings. Suddenly one broke under the intense vibrations. I stopped, shuddering at the incisive snap of the metallic cord. It fell silent but, like a melodious wave undulating through all its phases, the most distant harmonics sorrowfully responded and echoed for a long time. Then the airborne wave became subtly attenuated. Everything returns to somnolescence. The silence, torn apart for only an instant, returns, and envelopes me with fear and my solitude.] This entire episode recalls a metaphor used by Schopenhauer in the supplement to his discussion of music. "When . . . in reality and its terrors, it is our *will itself* that is roused and tormented . . . we are now ourselves the trembling string that is stretched and twanged" ("On the Metaphysics of Music," *The World as Will and Idea,* III, 237). It can be no mere coincidence that Gide expanded precisely this metaphor in the episode in question. Music, for Schopenhauer, was the art form par excellence, and Gide reflects this attitude throughout the *Cahiers.*

13. *Les Cahiers, OC,* I, 137. The biblical quotation is from Hebrews XII:1: "Compassed about with so great a cloud of witnesses."

Notes (Chapter II)

14. The "besetting sin" is sloth, or lapsing into the bad practices of Judaism. See Hebrews XII:1ff.
15. *Les Cahiers, OC*, I, 137. [METAPHORICAL; HUGO. Invisible lights hover about us, in what we believe to be the black night; souls shine like candles, souls already dead or yet unborn; immaterial space shimmers with lights—and man is surrounded by infinite legions spaced out all the way to God. . . . On azure field, great angels bow in contemplation.]
16. *Ibid., OC*, I, 128. [The least vibration of a soul long disturbs the spaces around it; the slightest cries awaken far distant echoes. The mysterious relationships between things cannot be altered with impunity; nothing becomes extinct. . . . It is the refrain of some primitive song of ecstasy which thus carries off my soul towards unknown devotions.]
17. *Ibid., OC*, I, 138. [And it is this that sometimes makes us aware of being moved by mysterious tendernesses; it is because a random harmony in the air has made our souls vibrate, a subtle, imperceptible melody in the soul has awakened some hidden alliteration.]
18. Walter began having visions as early as the first of August. The episode in question occurred at midnight, August 28. See *Les Cahiers, OC*, I, 114.
19. *Ibid., OC*, I, 125.
20. Schopenhauer, I, 324.
21. *Les Cahiers, OC*, I, 135. [*Not the color, only the nuance.* Therefore it is the relationship between words, no longer the sentence as a whole.]
22. *Si le Grain ne meurt, JAG*, II, 522. [How could I have understood, at the time, that (this crisis) was a personal one?]
23. *Les Cahiers, OC*, I, 118. Entry made August 6.
24. *Ibid., OC*, I, 122. The verses are from Genesis VIII:5 and Psalms LXI:2.
    And the tops of the mountains reappeared.
    Lead me to the rock that is beyond my reach.
25. *Ibid., OC*, I, 123. The verse is from I Corinthians III:13. [Each man's work shall be made manifest.]
26. Schopenhauer, I, 325.
27. Gide had deliberately chosen Barrès' publisher for his first book. See the letter to Mme Gide from her son, dated October 19, 1890, and reproduced in Delay, I, 469f.

Notes (Chapter II)

28. Delay, II, 37.
29. Gide-Valéry, *Correspondance* (Paris: Gallimard, 1955), p. 46. Dated January 26, 1891. [It is evolving terribly in me. . . . (I) had set myself up as the apostle of new truths, artistic truths, of course, truths opposed to yours. I had thought I was already a thorough symbolist. . . . Since then everything has changed. Mallarmé, above all, is the cause. (These theories) seem to be a direct apology for my book if they are not copies of its very sentences. Thus, I am a symbolist, and I'll have you know it.]
30. *JAG*, I, 21. Entry dated June 10, 1891.
31. See "Réponse à une enquête de la *Renaissance* sur le classicisme," *OC*, X, 23, and "Billet à Angèle," *OC*, XI, 39.
32. Gide-Valéry, *Correspondance*, p. 134. Dated November 3, 1891.
33. *Le Traité du Narcisse*, *OC*, I, 215. [Truths lie behind Form-Symbols. Every phenomenon is the Symbol of a Truth. Its sole duty is to manifest it; its sole sin, to prefer itself.]
34. *Ibid.*, *OC*, I, 217. [The pious Poet contemplates; he bends over the symbols and silently descends deep into the heart of things—and when he, the visionary, has perceived the Idea, the intimate and harmonious Number of its Being, which sustains the imperfect form, he seizes it and, heedless of the ephemeral form that invested it in time's flow, he is then able to give it again an eternal form, its own true and, in fact, fated Form—paradisiac and crystalline.]
35. In Jean Schlumberger, *Madeleine et André Gide* (Paris: Gallimard, 1956), p. 72.
36. *Les Cahiers*, *OC*, I, 94f. [Not at all a realistic truth, which is inevitably contingent; but a theoretical truth, which is absolute—at least on human terms. Ideal, as Taine defines it, that is, where the idea appears completely pure. It must stand out forcefully in the work. It is a demonstration.]
37. *Le Traité du Narcisse*, *OC*, I, 219.
38. *Ibid.*, *OC*, I, 217. See Gide's footnote to Part III: "Is it clear that I mean by symbol *all that appears*."
39. *Ibid.*, *OC*, I, 217. [. . . Where rhythmical and balanced sentences, symbols too, but pure symbols, in which words become transparent and revealing.]
40. Gide-Valéry, *Correspondance*, p. 99. Dated June 17, 1891. [The book is not *necessary*. So why then must we have books? . . .

Notes (Chapter III)

Hieroglyphics are enough to murmur the secrets of an entire science. . . . But we prostitute ourselves because we have loved the weak too much and because we *explain* out of love for them.]
41. Germaine Brée, *André Gide, l'insaisissable Protée* (Paris: Belles-Lettres, 1953), p. 41.
42. December 9, 1891. Quoted in Delay, II, 123.

CHAPTER III

1. We recall the heavy, yet innocent, sensual overtones given the compound *sympathein* in *Les Cahiers*. See above, pp. 32f., and *Les Cahiers, OC*, I, 34, 55.

   In the following discussion of *Le Voyage d'Urien*, I follow the chapter headings suggested by Gide, which have not been entirely respected in either the *OC* or the Pléiade volume, *Romans*: "Prélude./I.—Voyage sur l'océan pathétique./II.—La Mer des Sargasses./III.—Voyage vers une mer glaciale./Envoi." *JAG*, I, 966 (January 9, 1930).
2. *Le Voyage d'Urien, OC*, I, 363. [And still kneeling, we searched on the black water for the reflection of the sky I dream of.]
3. See Rimbaud's letter to George Izambard dated May 13, 1871, in Rimbaud, *Oeuvres*, ed. Suzanne Bernard (Paris: Garnier, 1960), p. 344.
4. See O'Brien, *Portrait of André Gide*, pp. 83f., and Delay, II, 172ff.
5. See Delay, II, 200ff., and especially Albert Guerard, *André Gide* (Cambridge, Mass.: Harvard University Press, 1951), pp. 58ff.
6. See Delay, II, 175.
7. "Préface pour une seconde édition du *Voyage d'Urien*," *Mercure de France*, XII (décembre, 1894), pp. 354ff.; reprinted in A. Gide, *Romans, récits et soties, oeuvres lyriques*, Bibliothèque de la Pléiade (Paris: Gallimard, 1958), pp. 1464f.
8. *JAG*, I, 308.
9. *Le Traité du Narcisse, OC*, I, 215.
10. *Romans*, p. 1464. [. . . It has been in existence for as long as all the things that manifest it. Its own mystical life consists in being consented to by men . . . its life . . . is the very need to manifest itself.]
11. *Ibid.* [It still seems right to me that an emotion which has been inspired by a landscape can use the landscape again, *like a word*, and flow back entirely into it, since originally the emotion was

contained by it. Emotion and landscape will no longer be bound by a cause and effect relationship, but rather, by an indefinable connection in which there is no longer a creditor or debtor, by an association of word and idea, of body and soul, of God and all appearance.]

12. *Ibid.* [We have here a sort of aesthetic algebra: emotion and its manifestation form an equation, one equals the other. When one says *emotion*, he will also say *landscape;* and when one reads *landscape*, he should thereupon know the *emotion*.]

13. See "Of the Pathetic Fallacy," *Modern Painters*, III, Chapter 12.

14. Schopenhauer, *The World as Will and Idea*, I, 324. The lines are from "Childe Harold's Pilgrimage," Canto III, l. 640f.

15. Entry made on October 31, 1852. Henri-Frédéric Amiel, *Fragments d'un journal intime*, ed. Edmond Scherer, 11th ed. (Geneva: Georg et Cie., 1911), I, 62. The first edition was published in 1882-84. [. . . All these innumerable and marvelous symbols which forms, colors, plants, living creatures, the earth, and the sky furnish at every moment for the eye that can see them were for me all charming and striking. Holding a poetic wand, I had only to touch a phenomenon for it to recount its moral meaning. Any landscape whatsoever is a state of soul, and whoever reads both will be astonished to find resemblances in every detail.]

16. *Notes d'un voyage en Bretagne, OC*, I, 9. The *Notes* were first published in the review *La Wallonie* (June, July, August, 1891). [It seemed that the landscape was only a projected emanation of myself . . . inert and virtual, it lay dormant until I came, and I created it, step by step, by perceiving its harmonies; I was its very consciousness.]

17. *JAG*, I, 28. The journal entry was made on January 1, 1892. Gide had first met Wilde in November, 1891. See Delay, II, 132, 151.

18. Ernest Renan, *De l'Origine du langage* (Paris: Calmann-Lévy, 1858), p. 121.

19. See *Le Voyage d'Urien, OC*, I, 290, 331.

20. *Les Poésies d'André Walter* were written for the most part during the summer of 1891, at the same time as *Le Traité du Narcisse*. An earlier poem, "Nuit de Prière," changed to "Nuit d'Idumée," was begun in January and sent to Valéry in March, 1891. See Gide-Valéry, *Correspondance*, pp. 47, 59f., and Delay, II, 103.

21. *Les Poésies d'André Walter, OC*, I, 180. [A new lamp replaces

the empty:/One night succeeds another;/And one hears slip away
in the night/The sound of the melancholy hourglass./We patch up
false syllogisms/And we quibble over the Trinity./But this is less
than lyrical/And our lamps yield little light.]

22. *Le Voyage d'Urien, OC,* I, 281. It is likely that Gide's lamp is a
close descendant of Baudelaire's image in the opening stanza of
"Le Voyage." As Walter adopted lines from "Recueillement,"
Gide undoubtedly assimilated his predecessor's image and expanded its undertones in the first pages of Urien's logbook. [With-
out my having noticed it, my lamp went out; my window lay
open in the dawn.]

23. *Les Cahiers d'André Walter, OC,* I, 108.

24. *Ibid., OC,* I, 168; "Bluffy, the name of a glacier, of an avalanche,
a blue descent into the snow."

25. *Les Poésies d'André Walter, OC,* I, 191.

26. *Le Voyage d'Urien, OC,* I, 306f. [Ice water, who can describe
your purity? . . . It was as pure and intoxicating as early morn-
ing mountain air . . . it washed away the fever's blemishes and
its delicate strength seeped into our thoughts like lustral water.]

27. *Les Poésies d'André Walter, OC,* I, 197. [Our bare feet have sunk
in the mud./Oh, stain on the delicate skin!—a bit of clear water/
To steep the bare feet in a wave of the sea.]

28. *Ibid., OC,* 198. [I think it would be best for us/To try to go back
to sleep.]

29. O'Brien, *Portrait of André Gide,* pp. 78, 83, and see Renée Lang,
André Gide et la pensée allemande (Paris: Egloff, 1949), pp. 71f.
Gide acknowledges his debt to Novalis in a footnote to Chapter
VI of the "Voyage sur l'océan pathétique." He transplanted onto
the beach of one of the islands visited by his mariners Novalis'
figure of a young boy writing mysterious signs on the sand.

30. *Le Voyage d'Urien, OC,* I, 291. [The stifling perfumes which rose
from every island and which the wind beat down upon us, the
perfumes which dizzied us would, I believe, have killed us. They
were so dense that we could see clouds of aroma swirling.]

31. *Ibid., OC,* I, 292.

32. *Ibid., OC,* I, 295.

33. *Ibid., OC,* I, 302.

34. Delay, II, 200.

35. *Le Voyage d'Urien, OC,* I, 296.

36. Brée, *André Gide, l'insaisissable Protée*, p. 47.
37. Gide-Valéry, *Correspondance*, p. 179f.
38. Stephen Ullmann, *The Image in the Modern French Novel* (Cambridge, Eng.: Cambridge University Press, 1960), p. 13.
39. Brée, *André Gide, l'insaisissable Protée*, p. 50.

CHAPTER IV

1. *La Tentative amoureuse* was composed in part at Yport, the summer home of the Laurens family, during the month of June, 1893, and finished at La Roque in September. It was with Paul-Albert Laurens that Gide made his first trip to North Africa.
2. *La Tentative amoureuse*, *OC*, I, 223. [Our books will not be very truthful accounts of ourselves but rather of our plaintive desires, the longing for other lives forever forbidden, and for all impossible gestures . . . each book is no more than a deferred temptation.] See also *Romans*, p. 71.
3. *JAG*, I, 41. Gide is referring in particular to *La Tentative*. [The active subject is oneself; the retroactive object is a subject one imagines. We have here, then, an indirect method of acting upon oneself; and it is also simply a story.]
4. O'Brien, *Portrait of André Gide*, p. 89.
5. *La Tentative amoureuse*, *OC*, I, 238f.
6. "Desire is like a brilliant flame, and whatever it touches turns only to ashes—a light dust which a little breeze can scatter—let us think, then, only of the eternal." This quotation from Calderón de la Barca's *La Vida es sueño* stands as epigraph to *La Tentative* and, also, as the theme of its final meditation. *OC*, I, 222.
7. "Lettre à M. Scheffer," *OC*, IV, 616. Undated. [How many buds we carry within ourselves . . . that never blossom except in our books! . . . My formula for creating a hero is quite simple: take one of these buds, put it in a flower-pot, all alone; within a short time, an admirable individual will appear.]
8. *La Tentative amoureuse*, *OC*, I, 226.
9. In both works long, aimless walks evoke, by their repetition and inconclusiveness, the state of mind of each couple. Dissatisfied with their relationship, yet unable to bring it to a satisfactory conclusion and thus go beyond their present stagnant situation, they strive vaguely for something else that their relationship does not provide. This "something else" is suggested by the presence in

174

both works of a holy place, a brilliantly-lighted and isolated church in *Les Poésies* and a walled-in garden, equally isolated in *La Tentative amoureuse*. Each place is inaccessible to the lovers so long as they are together.

10. *La Tentative amoureuse, OC,* I, 234. [On their return, Rachel found on the sand an enormous black and elastic cuttlefish egg with so strange and almost deliberate a shape that they judged it important for them.]

11. *Ibid., OC,* I, 233.

12. "Lettre à Eugène Rouart," in Delay, II, 401.

13. Brée, *André Gide, l'insaisissable Protée,* p. 75.

14. *Paludes, OC,* I, 376. [I arrange facts in such a way as to make them conform more to truth than to reality . . . events are adapted to characters; that is what makes good novels; what happens to us is in no way made for others. By now, Hubert would have caught an enormous quantity of fish; Tityre does not catch a thing. That is psychological truth.]

15. See Gide's lecture prepared in the summer of 1901, "Les Limites de l'art," *OC,* III, 407.

16. "Lettre à Angèle" (June 15, 1899), *OC,* III, 197. [The work of art is a distillation. The artist is a one-man distiller. For one tiny drop of this fine alcohol, an enormous amount of life must be concentrated.]

17. *Paludes, OC,* I, 393.

18. *Ibid., OC,* I, 445.

19. *Ibid., OC,* I, 377.

20. *Ibid., OC,* I, 410. [*Paludes* . . . is the story of the neutral terrain, that which belongs to everyone . . . better still, it is the story of the normal man, the point of departure for each one of us—the story of the third person, about whom we speak, who lives in everyone, and who does not die with us. In Virgil, his name is Tityre and it is explicitly stated that he is reclining—"Tityre recubans."—*Paludes* is the story of the recumbent man.]

21. *Ibid., OC,* 413.

22. *Ibid., OC,* I, 412.

23. Many of Gide's major critical pieces revolve about this very relationship. "Nationalisme et littérature" (1909), is perhaps the most thorough single treatment of the problem; it recurs in "De l'influence en littérature" (1900) and, of course, in the Dostoievsky lectures (1923).

24. *Paludes, OC,* I, 387f.
25. "Lettre à M. Scheffer," *OC,* IV, 616f. Undated.
26. In *Si le Grain ne meurt,* Gide treats this period as the most confused of his life. This "period of dissipation and restlessness" ended finally with his departure for North Africa in late 1893. See *JAG,* II, 529.

CHAPTER V

1. See Gide's remarks concerning *Les Nourritures terrestres* and the Symbolists in *Journal des Faux-Monnayeurs, OC,* XIII, 37f., and *JAG,* I, 826.
2. In a journal entry made at the end of July, 1893, while he was at Yport, deleted from the published *Journal,* Gide confessed the following: "I think I'm going to abandon this book; it is definitely too tediously difficult." In Delay, II, 242.
3. *La Tentative amoureuse, OC,* I, 238f.
4. *JAG,* I, 40.
5. See "Lettre à Marcel Drouin" (Fall, 1894) in Yvonne Davet, *Autour des "Nourritures terrestres"* (Paris: Gallimard, 1948), pp. 55f., and "Lettre à Pierre Louÿs" (October 19, 1894) in Delay, II, 389.
6. In Delay, II, 388.
7. "Préface pour une seconde édition de *Paludes," Mercure de France,* XVI (November, 1895), 199. Reproduced in A. Gide, *Romans, récits et soties, oeuvres lyriques,* p. 1476. [. . . His life and ideas in accordance with the passionate optimism to which he had been led first by his temperament, then by his admiration for Goethe and the slow meditation of Leibniz.]
8. Henri Peyre, "André Gide et les problèmes d'influence en littérature," *Modern Language Notes,* LVII (November, 1942), 560.
9. *Si le Grain ne meurt, JAG,* II, 577.
10. Renée Lang, *André Gide et la pensée allemande,* p. 75.
11. *JAG,* I, 51.
12. Gide-Valéry, *Correspondance,* pp. 219f. ["A state of being can be willed without being free," Leibniz says, among other things. And it is commonplace enough. But what is not, is to strive, whether compelled or not, to make all of one's states a matter of volition. . . . My wisdom is there, and I say wisdom because that is what a formula for happiness is called.] See Leibnitz, *New*

Notes (Chapter V)

Essays concerning Human Understanding, trans. Alfred Gideon Langley (New York: Macmillan, 1896), p. 181. Hereafter abbreviated, *NE.* Echoes of these remarks occur at the same time in the *Journal:* "A clear understanding of God makes one want to follow the direction of things, the direction of oneself. The wise man lives without ethics, according to his wisdom." *JAG,* I, 54f. See also *JAG,* I, 52, 55.

13. *NE,* p. 203. See also *NE,* p. 166.
14. October, 1894, *JAG,* I, 55.
15. Leibniz's working definition of knowledge is "simply the perception of the connection and agreement, or of the opposition and disagreement, which we find between *two of our ideas." NE,* p. 397.
16. *NE,* p. 81.
17. See Gide's approval of Lessing's parable in a journal entry dated October, 1894, *JAG,* I, 52. Truths such as Gide was seeking, Leibniz suggested, are derivable only from the senses since they depend upon examples; so their universal necessity can never be sufficiently established. Mathematics, logic, metaphysics, and ethics, however, "are full of such truths, and consequently their proof can only come from internal principles which are called innate." *NE,* p. 44.
18. *JAG,* I, 94. [I maintain that an artist must have a special world to which he alone has the key. It is not enough to offer something new, although that alone is quite an accomplishment; but everything in him should be or seem new, transparent behind a highly coloring idiosyncracy.

    He must have a particular philosophy, aesthetics, ethics; his entire work tends only to result in revealing these. And that is what makes his style. I have also discovered, and this is very important, that he has to have a particular way of joking, a particular sense of humor.] In a letter to his mother dated October, 1894, Gide insisted upon the same point, stating that the artist is by definition an exception to all rules. In Delay, II, 386.
19. *JAG,* I, 89. [. . . To consider only the distinct and unique part of each being, of which the common substance is only the too massive support.]
20. "Chroniques de *L'Ermitage"* (February, 1905), *OC,* IV, 389f. [The recipe for the right way to live and think had been discovered.

We had inherited from the Romans a just and beautiful image of man upon which we had modeled ourselves without first having been able to realize that perhaps it did not fully express our essence: it seemed that we had to limit ourselves to it. . . . Nothing foreign was accepted except what reminded us of this image. . . . Why, of course, everything has been said during the seven thousand years there have been men "who think"—but for the yawning gulf of years during which there have been brutes *who do not think*, who had not yet begun to think, how many things remained to be said.]

21. In *Littérature et morale* Gide considers "humanity as the realization of possible relationships. The almost infinite number of possible relationships assures humanity an almost infinite duration." *JAG*, I, 91.

22. *JAG*, I, 56.

23. *Littérature et morale*, *JAG*, I, 87.

24. *JAG*, I, 54, 55f. [. . . Can very well flatter one's pride and serve poetry; but it is not *rational*. A clear understanding of God makes one want to follow the direction of things, the direction of oneself. . . . The laws of nature are those of God . . . they are in us. . . . He who submits to them willingly is the wise man; nature submits the fools to them.]

25. *Littérature et morale*, *JAG*, I, 92.

26. It is true that, in *Si le Grain ne meurt*, Gide uses the term "représenter" in reproducing a remark of his made in 1891. See *JAG*, II, 542. In all probability he used, at the time, the term "manifester" instead; such a lapse in memory can be attributed to the fact that the memoirs were written long after he had abandoned a mystical vocabulary.

27. *Littérature et morale*, *JAG*, I, 91.

28. Gide quotes Leibniz in support of this thesis: "Is it not true that truths are posterior to the ideas from which they are born?" *JAG*, I, 52. See also Leibniz, *NE*, p. 82.

29. *JAG*, I, 55. Entry of October, 1894. See *JAG*, I, 52.

30. *Littérature et morale*, *JAG*, I, 91.

31. *Ibid.*, *JAG*, I, 92. [Time and space are the stage where, with the help of our brains, innumerable truths are posed for their own performance; and we play our roles like marionettes, willing, convinced, devoted, and extremely sensual. I see no reason to be

sad about this; on the contrary, I am pleased with this conviction about my role. On the whole and if everything warrants it, it is good that each one alone discovers this role.]

32. *Ibid., JAG*, I, 94. [In studying the question of a work of art's justification, one finds that this sufficient reason, the symbol of the work, is its composition.

A well-composed work is necessarily symbolical. Around what would its components group themselves and what would guide their arrangement if not the idea of the work which makes its arrangement symbolical?

The work of art is an idea which is exaggerated.

It is around the symbol that a book is composed.

The sentence is an excrescence of an idea.

THEORY. Things are in a perpetual disequilibrium; hence their flow.

Equilibrium is perfect "health," what Taine calls a happy accident; but it cannot be realized physically because of what we said; it is realizable only in the work of art. The work of art is an equilibrium outside of time, an artificial health.]

33. See "Projet de préface pour *La Porte étroite*," *Feuillets, OC*, VI, 359.

34. *Le Traité du Narcisse, OC*, I, 218f.

35. *Ibid., OC*, I, 207f.

36. *JAG*, I, 33. Entry dated November, 1892.

37. In Delay, II, 263. Entry dated April, 1893. [She feared sensuality as something that was too strong and that could kill her. I assure you, it is *like the dread of death*.]

38. *Feuillets* (1897–1902), *JAG*, I, 102. [Precipitate sensuality. (His haste was such that he skinned his hands on the doorlock.)]

39. One can also consider, in this light, the brief configuration of *La Porte étroite* in the journal of October, 1894. "Possibility for anguish: the soul that believes it has insufficiently adored." *JAG*, I, 55.

40. *Feuillets* (1893), *JAG*, I, 49. [With me, the idea of a work often precedes its *imagination* by several years.

As soon as the idea of a work has taken form, that is, as soon as the work becomes organized, its elaboration consists in little more than suppressing all that is useless to its *organism*.]

41. "Lettre à Angèle" (October, 1898), *OC*, III, 166.

42. *Feuillets* (1921), *JAG*, I, 716. See *JAG*, I, 49.
43. "Lettre à Angèle" (October, 1898), *OC*, III, 164f.
44. *Ibid.* It is true that Gide made a similar statement years earlier in a letter to Valéry (November 3, 1891, *Correspondance*, p. 134). The insistence upon the new attitude towards life that an artist brings distinguishes the earlier statement from the other two mentioned here and above. Gide always believed in the individuality of the true artist, but at the time of *Le Traité du Narcisse*, his individuality was attributed to different causes. He distinguished himself from the masses because he was able to see the true reality, he was a visionary. His particular philosophy, aesthetic, etc., enabled him to approach and express this absolute in a way commensurate with his own personality. For in him, in his soul, lay the ultimate explanation of things. The purpose of *Littérature et morale* was, we have seen, to emancipate Gide not only from "an absolute faith," as Germaine Brée observes (*André Gide, l'insaisissable Protée*, p. 357), but from a belief in an absolute realm of truth.
45. *JAG*, I, 56. For a development of this idea see "Lettres à Mme Gide" (October, 1894), in Delay, II, 386ff., 393. The formula was later fully developed in *Les Nourritures terrestres* (1897), where, in large type, it occupies a prominent place in the early pages. See *Les Nourritures terrestres*, *OC*, II, 67.

CHAPTER VI

1. *Littérature et morale*, *JAG*, I, 90f.
2. *Ibid.*, *JAG*, I, 88.
3. *Ibid.*, *JAG*, I, 87: "Thus things in nature vibrate to the approach of sound only when they themselves are capable, with the help of the impact, of producing the sound." See *Les Cahiers*, *OC*, I, 137f.
4. *JAG*, I, 257.
5. See *Journal des Faux-Monnayeurs*, *OC*, XIII, 48f., and *JAG*, I, 358, 830.
6. It was to this point that Madeleine was especially sensitive in her criticism of *Le Traité du Narcisse*. She felt that his represented ideas might jell in the mind and deeds of an impressionable reader. See *Journal de Madeleine* in Jean Schlumberger, *Madeleine et André Gide*, p. 73. Michel of *L'Immoraliste* might be con-

sidered as such an impressionable disciple. Easily convinced of Menalque's ethic, he proved unable to live by it with the same sangfroid and thus precipitated himself and Marceline to disaster.

7. *JAG*, I, 55. [It is not good to tempt others. God sends each one temptations commensurate with his strength; it is bad and unwise to provide people with those they cannot overcome. That is why inept instruction is dangerous, why one should not cry out one's ideas too loudly, for fear the weak might hear.

The truth can be told to everyone; ideas, only in proportion to each person's strength.]

8. "De l'Influence en littérature," *OC*, III, 272.

9. *Littérature et morale, JAG*, I, 90. [Analysis must precede synthesis; and analysis, a need of the spirit, arises from the feeling of complexity. This feeling can become an impassioned stupefaction.]

10. *Ibid.* [Individual characters are more general (I mean, more human) than ethnic characters. That is, man insofar as he is an individual tries to escape his race. And as soon as he no longer represents his race, he represents man. The idiosyncracy is a pretext for generalities.]

11. *Paludes, OC*, I, 412. [. . . You will certainly understand me better if you think of all the enormous landscape that appears through a keyhole the moment your eye comes close enough to the door. He who sees no more than the lock, could see the whole world if he only knew enough to stoop down. It suffices that the possibility of generalization exists; it is then up to the reader or the critic to make the generalization.]

12. *JAG*, I, 41.

13. Camille Mauclair, "Paludes," *Mercure de France*, XV (July, 1895), 102f.

14. From an unpublished letter in the Bibliothèque Littéraire Jacques Doucet, quoted in part in Michel Décaudin, *La Crise des valeurs symbolistes, vingt ans de poésie française, 1895–1914* (Toulouse: Privat, 1960), p. 52.

15. Preface to *Le Roi Candaule, OC*, III, 295.

16. "L'Evolution du théâtre," *OC*, IV, 205.

17. See *Paludes, OC*, I, 376, and above, Chapter IV.

18. "Lettre à Marcel Drouin" (Fall, 1894), quoted in Davet, *Autour des "Nourritures terrestres,"* pp. 55f., and "Lettre à Pierre Louÿs" (October 19, 1894), quoted in Delay, II, 389.

19. "Considérations sur la mythologie grecque," *OC*, IX, 147ff. First published in March, 1919.
20. *JAG*, I, 996. Entry dated July 8, 1930.
21. "L'Evolution du théâtre," *OC*, IV, 211, 214. [The individual did not become banal by compulsion, but pushed himself to his limits out of virtue; each required from himself only himself and, without becoming deformed, attached himself to a god. Hence the great number of gods, as numerous as men's instincts. . . . For them religion did not erect atop a cross or upon the earth this bundle of virtues or that moral specter which one had to resemble under threat of being held impious. The typical man was not unique but legion; or rather, there was no typical man.]
22. In Léon Pierre-Quint, *André Gide* (Paris: Stock, 1952), p. 391. The interview is dated December, 1927.
23. Louis Martin-Chauffier, "Notices," *OC*, XIII, xf.
24. "Considérations sur la mythologie grecque," *OC*, IX, 150.
25. "Lettre d'André Gide à François Mauriac," *La Table Ronde*, no. 61 (January, 1953), p. 93. The date of this letter is July 1, 1922.
26. Rudolf Arnheim, "The Robin and the Saint: on the twofold nature of the artistic image," *The Journal of Aesthetics and Art Criticism*, XVIII (September, 1959), 74ff. In this article Arnheim analyzes the semantic properties of the image, reducing them, in the ideal work, to these two mutually dependent elements: self-image and likeness.
27. "De l'influence en littérature," *OC*, III, 269: "The true artist seeks the man behind the work, and it is from him that he learns."
28. *Propositions*, *OC*, VI, 353f.
29. See "Lettres à Angèle," *OC*, III, 220.
30. Arnheim, "The Robin and the Saint," pp. 78f.
31. Albert Thibaudet, *Histoire de la littérature française de 1789 à nos jours* (Paris: Stock, 1936), p. 445. Brée, *André Gide, l'insaisissable Protée*, p. 362.
32. Thibaudet, *Histoire*, p. 139.
33. Jean-Michel Hennebert, "Du *Prométhée* à l'art d'André Gide," *Prétexte*, no. 1 (February 15, 1952), p. 71.
34. George A. Buttrick, *The Parables of Jesus* (New York: Harper, 1928), p. xv. Consider also Harry Levin's observation: "Plato's myths are notable examples of argument reverting to parable," in "Some Meanings of Myth," *Myth and Myth-Making*, ed. Henry A. Murray (New York: George Braziller, 1960), p. 105.

Notes (Chapter VII)

35. C. M. Bowra, *The Greek Experience* (New York: World, 1959), pp. 115, 117f.
36. See *ibid.*, p. 115.
37. Buttrick, *The Parables of Jesus*, p. xv.
38. Charles Harold Dodd, *The Parables of the Kingdom*, revised ed. (New York: Scribner, 1961), pp. 10f.
39. *Journal des Faux-Monnayeurs*, OC, XIII, 15. In a letter to Marcel Drouin dated May 10, 1894, Gide says that the writer's conclusions must be questions addressed to the reader, that the writer must corner his reader and force him to answer. In Davet, *Autour des "Nourritures terrestres,"* pp. 66f.
40. These remarks suggest another trait Gide's parables have in common with their biblical predecessors. The aim of both is to teach. Gide's "côté didactique" can be discovered in all of his works, even in the "soties" where it is disguised by farce. For a long discussion of Gide's didacticism, see Max Marchand, *Le Complexe pédagogique et didactique d'André Gide* (Oran: Fouque, 1954).
41. *Cf. Si le Grain ne meurt*, JAG, II, 497, and I, 859.
42. Erich Auerbach, *Mimesis* (Garden City, N.Y.: Doubleday, 1957), p. 12.
43. B. T. D. Smith, *The Parables of the Synoptic Gospels* (Cambridge, Eng.: Cambridge University Press, 1937), pp. 3, 33.

CHAPTER VII

1. Earlier in the same interview, Angèle immediately places herself in Tityre's situation. "That would have frightened me," she says after hearing a description of Tityre's swamp at night. *Paludes*, OC, I, 375.
2. Dodd, *The Parables of the Kingdom*, pp. 5, 10.
3. *Le Prométhée mal enchaîné*, OC, III, 147.
4. *Ibid.*, OC, III, 157.
5. See JAG, I, 18, 20.
6. *Philoctète*, OC, III, 63.
7. In Delay, II, 666. [The novel must now prove that it can be other than a mirror carried along a road, that it can be superior and a priori; that is, deduced; that is, composed; that is, a work of art. . . .]
8. Mauclair admitted that the notion of "ideoréalisme" came to him from Johann Fichte. The artistic counterpart of idealism, it can-

183

not create an art but an artistic consciousness. It involves the perception of ideas committed to a plastic medium, whereas idealism considers ideas in themselves; "one completes and justifies the other." See Camille Mauclair, *Eleusis, causeries sur la cité intérieure* (Paris: Perrin, 1894), p. 110.

9. In Delay, II, 667f. [We are rabid apriorists. I have a fair hope that the novel will prove it. . . . The novel will prove that it can depict something other than reality, that it can depict emotion and thought directly. It will show to what extent it can be deduced, *before the experience of things*; that is, to what extent it can be composed; that is to say, a work of art. It will show that it can be a work of art, fully composed, with a realism not of small and contingent facts, but superior, with ideorealism as Mauclair used to say; that it is more real, more truthful than the things of so-called reality, as the triangle in mathematics is more real and truthful than the imperfect triangles of surveyors. In their relationship, each part of a work must prove the truth of every other, and no other proof is necessary. There is nothing more irritating than the evidence Mr. Gourmont gives for everything he puts forth—he has seen! he has heard! as though proof by reality were necessary. As though the world of the mind differed somehow from the world of things, and the microcosm were governed by laws other than those of the macrocosm. One is certain, the other, uncertain . . . that is the whole difference.]

10. *Les Cahiers d'André Walter, OC,* I, 95.

11. Germaine Brée suggests that the theoretical part of *Les Cahiers* was written after the book, since there is in reality little rapport between the two. This might explain why Walter's theories do not apply to his book but do apply to Gide's *Le Traité.* See Brée, *André Gide, l'insaisissable Protée*, p. 38, and above, Chapter II.

12. It should be made clear that the term "realism" applied to Gide's fiction is purely relative. The "récits" are more realistic than the "soties" and myths but are by no means comparable to the works of Balzac or Zola. We take the term to mean the degree to which an artificial construction—such as a work of art—can be recognized as a description of something belonging, at least potentially, to our world.

13. *JAG,* I, 55, 102; "Lettre à M. Deherme" (May 19, 1911), *OC,* VI, 470; and *Feuillets, OC,* XIII, 439f.

14. *L'Immoraliste*, OC, IV, 16.
15. *Ibid.*, OC, IV, 168f.
16. *La Symphonie pastorale*, OC, IX, 87.
17. See OC, XIII, 439, and OC, VI, 470.
18. *La Porte étroite*, OC, V, 238.
19. *Ibid.*, OC, V, 241: "If I were to marry another woman, I could only pretend to love her."
20. *Ibid.*
21. Gustave Flaubert, *Oeuvres complètes: Correspondance 1847–1852* (Paris: Conard, 1926), II, 398.
22. The word "monographe" was used in the sense of "récit" by Gide himself. See *JAG*, I, 686 (November 23, 1921). For indications of Gide's own awareness of the "poly-monographic" structure of *Les Faux-Monnayeurs*, see *JAG*, I, 879 (April 17, 1928).
23. See OC, XI, 149 and O'Brien, *Portrait of André Gide*, pp. 196f.
24. For two such interpretations see Elizabeth R. Jackson, "The Evanescent World of the *Faux-Monnayeurs*," *Symposium*, XVI (Summer, 1962), 103–13, and Wylie Sypher, "Gide's Cubist Novel," *Kenyon Review*, XI (Spring, 1949), 291–309.

A Selected Bibliography

Works by André Gide

Attendu que . . . (Alger: Charlot, 1943).
Correspondance Francis Jammes et André Gide, 1893–1938,
 ed. Robert Mallet (Paris: Gallimard, 1948).
Correspondance Paul Claudel et André Gide, 1899–1926,
 ed. Robert Mallet (Paris: Gallimard, 1949).
Correspondance Paul Valéry et André Gide, 1890–1942,
 ed. Robert Mallet (Paris: Gallimard, 1955).
Divers: Caractères, Un Esprit non prévenu, Dictées, Lettres
 (Paris: Gallimard, 1931).
Eloges (Neuchâtel: Ides et Calendes, 1948).
Feuillets d'automne (Paris: Mercure de France, 1949).
Interviews imaginaires (New York: Pantheon, 1943).
 Imaginary Interviews, trans. with an introduction by
 Malcolm Cowley (New York: Alfred A. Knopf, 1944).
Journal, 1889–1949, Souvenirs, Bibliothèque de la Pléiade, 2
 vols. (Paris: Gallimard, 1948–1954).
"Lettres à François Mauriac," *La Table ronde,* no. 61
 (janvier, 1953), 91–106.
Lettres à un sculpteur (Paris: Marcel Sautier, 1952).
Lettres de Charles du Bos et réponses d'André Gide (Paris:
 Corréa, 1950).
Littérature engagée, ed. Yvonne Davet (Paris: Gallimard,
 1950).
Morceaux choisis (Paris: Gallimard, 1921).

A Selected Bibliography

Oeuvres complètes d'André Gide, 15 vols. (Paris: Gallimard, 1932–1939).

Poétique (Neuchâtel: Ides et Calendes, 1947).

Préfaces (Neuchâtel: Ides et Calendes, 1948).

"Quelques réflexions sur l'abandon du sujet dans les arts plastiques," *Verve,* I (décembre, 1937), 7–10.

Rencontres (Neuchâtel: Ides et Calendes, 1948).

Le Retour de l'enfant prodigue, précedé de cinq autres traités (Paris: Gallimard, 1912).

Le Retour, suivi de lettres à Raymond Bonheur (Neuchâtel: Ides et Calendes, 1946).

Romans, récits et soties, oeuvres lyriques, Bibliothèque de la Pléiade (Paris: Gallimard, 1958).

Théâtre complet, 8 vols. (Neuchâtel: Ides et Calendes, 1947–1949).

Studies on André Gide

BOOKS:

Albérès, René Marill, *L'Odyssée d'André Gide* (Paris: La Nouvelle Edition, 1951).

Ames, Van Meter, *André Gide* (Norfolk, Conn.: New Directions, 1947).

Archambault, Paul, *Humanité d'André Gide* (Paris: Bloud et Gay, 1946).

Beigbeder, Marc, *André Gide* (Paris: Editions universelles, 1954).

Brachfeld, George I., *André Gide and the Communist Temptation* (Geneva: E. Droz; Paris: Minard, 1959).

Brée, Germaine, *André Gide, l'insaisissable Protée* (Paris: Belles-lettres, 1953).

———, *Gide* (New Brunswick, N.J.: Rutgers University Press, 1963).

A Selected Bibliography

Davet, Yvonne, *Autour des "Nourritures terrestres"* (Paris: Gallimard, 1948).

Delay, Jean, *La Jeunesse d'André Gide*, 2 vols. (Paris: Gallimard, 1956, 1957).

Fayer, H. M., *Gide, Freedom and Dostoievsky* (Burlington, Vt.: Lane Press, 1946).

Fowlie, Wallace, *André Gide: His Life and Art* (New York: Macmillan, 1965).

Guerard, Albert J., *André Gide* (Cambridge, Mass.: Harvard University Press, 1951).

Hytier, Jean, *André Gide*, trans. Richard Howard (Garden City, N.Y.: Doubleday, 1962).

Ireland, G. W., *André Gide* (New York: Grove Press, 1963).

Iseler, Paul, *Les Débuts d'André Gide vus par Pierre Louÿs* (Paris: Editions du Sagittaire, 1937).

Lang, Renée, *André Gide et la pensée allemande* (Paris: Egloff, 1949).

Martin, Claude, *André Gide par lui-même* (Paris: Editions du Seuil, 1963).

Martin du Gard, Roger, *Notes sur André Gide* (Paris: Gallimard, 1951).

Mondor, Henri, *Les Premiers Temps d'une amitié: André Gide et Paul Valéry* (Monaco: Editions du Rocher, 1947).

Naville, Arnold, *Bibliographie des écrits d'André Gide* (Paris: H. Matarasso, 1949).

O'Brien, Justin, *Portrait of André Gide, A Critical Biography* (New York: Alfred A. Knopf, 1953).

Pierre-Quint, Léon, *André Gide* (Paris: Stock, 1952).

Savage, Catharine H., *André Gide: l'evolution de sa pensée religieuse* (Paris: Nizet, 1962).

Schlumberger, Jean, *Madeleine et André Gide* (Paris: Gallimard, 1956).

Thierry, Jean-Jacques, *André Gide* (Paris: Gallimard, 1962).

Ullmann, Stephen, *The Image in the Modern French Novel* (Cambridge, Eng.: Cambridge University Press, 1960).

ARTICLES:

Bernstein, Henry, *et al.*, *Hommage à André Gide, études, souvenirs, témoignages* (Paris: Editions du Capitole, 1928).

Blanchot, Maurice, "Gide et la littérature de l'expérience," *L'Arche*, IV (janvier, 1947), 87–98.

Brée, Germaine, "Form and Content in Gide," *French Review*, XXX (May, 1957), 423–28.

——, "Signification du *Prométhée mal enchaîné* et sa place dans l'oeuvre de Gide," *French Review*, XXVI (October, 1952), 13–20.

Etiemble, René, "Le Style du *Thésée* d'André Gide," *Les Temps modernes*, II (mars, 1947), 1032–38.

Fowlie, Wallace, "The Fountain and the Thirst: André Gide," in *Essays in Modern Literary Criticism*, ed. Ray B. West (New York: Rinehart, 1952), pp. 489–501.

Freedman, Ralph, "Imagination and Form in André Gide: *La Porte étroite* and *La Symphonie pastorale*," *Accent*, XVII (Autumn, 1957), 217–28.

Ghéon, Henri, "André Gide," *Mercure de France*, XXII (mai, 1897), 237–62.

Holdheim, William W., "Gide's *Caves du Vatican* and the Illusionism of the Novel," *Modern Language Notes*, LXXVII (May, 1962), 292–304.

——, "Gide's *Paludes*: The Humor of Falsity," *French Review*, XXXII (April, 1959), 401–09.

——, "The Dual Structure of the *Prométhée mal enchaîné*," *Modern Language Notes*, LXXIV (December, 1959), 714–20.

A Selected Bibliography

Jackson, Elizabeth R., "The Evanescent World of the *Faux-Monnayeurs*," *Symposium*, XVI (Summer, 1962), 103–13.

Kanes, Martin, "Gide's Early Attitude to the Symbol, *Symposium*, XIII (Fall, 1959), 195–215.

Lang, Renée B. "Gide et Nietzsche," *Romanic Review*, XXXIV (April, 1943), 139–49.

Louria, Yvette, "Le Contenu latent du *Philoctète* gidien," *French Review*, XXV (April, 1952), 348–54.

McLaren, James C., *et al.*, "André Gide," *L'Esprit créateur*, I (Spring, 1961).

Magny, Claude-Edmonde, "A propos du *Thésée*: l'ethique secrète d'André Gide," *Poésie*, no. 36 (décembre, 1946), 82–94.

Malraux, André, "Aspects d'André Gide," *Action*, III (mars-avril, 1922), 17–21.

——, "*Les Nouvelles Nourritures*, par André Gide" *Nouvelle Revue française*, XLV (décembre, 1935), 935–37.

Marsh, Harold, "The Artist as Seer," *Yale French Studies*, no. 4 (1949), 44–54.

Martin, Claude, "Etat présent des études gidiennes," *Critique*, XX (juillet, 1964), 598–625.

Mauclair, Camille, "*Paludes*," *Mercure de France*, XV (juillet, 1895), 102–03.

O'Brien, Justin, "Additions to the Gide Bibliography," *Romanic Review*, XLIII (February, 1952), 34–53.

——, "Gide's *Nourritures terrestres* and Vergil's *Bucolics*," *Romanic Review*, XLIII (April, 1952), 117–25.

O'Nan, Martha, "Form in the Novel: André Gide and Roger Martin du Gard," *Symposium*, XII (Spring-Fall, 1958), 81–93.

O'Reilly, Robert F., "The Emergence of Gide's Art Form in *Paludes*," *Symposium*, XIX (Fall, 1965), 236–48.

Peyre, Henri, "André Gide et les problèmes d'influences en

littérature," *Modern Language Notes*, XVII (November, 1942), 558–67.

Picon, Gaëton, *et al.*, "André Gide," *Yale French Studies*, no. 7 (1950).

Rhodes, Solomon A., "The Influence of Walt Whitman on André Gide," *Romanic Review*, XXI (April, 1940), 156–71.

Roudiez, Leon, "*L'Etranger, La Chute* and the Aesthetic Legacy of Gide," *French Review*, XXXII (February, 1959), 300–10.

Schlumberger, Jean, *et al.*, "Hommage à André Gide," *Nouvelle Revue française* (novembre, 1951).

——, "Cahier André Gide," *Prétexte*, no. 1 (15 février 1952).

Solier, René de, "L'Esthétique de Gide," *Synthèses*, no. 83 (avril, 1953), 270–79.

Sypher, Wylie, "Gide's Cubist Novel," *Kenyon Review*, XI (Spring, 1949), 291–309.

Thibaudet, Albert, "Réflexions sur la littérature: le voyage intérieur," *Nouvelle Revue française*, XVII (1 septembre 1921), 329–37.

Wilkins, Burleigh Taylor, "*L'Immoraliste* Revisited," *Romanic Review*, LII (April, 1962), 112–27.

York, Ruth B., "Circular Patterns in Gide's 'Soties,'" *French Review*, XXXIV (February, 1961), 336–43.

General Reference

Amiel, Henri-Frédéric, *Fragments d'un journal intime*, ed. Edmond Scherer, 11th ed., 2 vols. (Geneva: H. Georg, 1911).

Arnheim, Rudolf, "The Robin and the Saint: on the twofold Nature of the Artistic Image," *Journal of Aesthetics and Art Criticism*, XVIII (September, 1959), 68–79.

A Selected Bibliography

Bowra, C. M., *The Heritage of Symbolism* (London: Macmillan, 1943).

Buttrick, George A., *The Parables of Jesus* (New York: Harper, 1928).

Clark, Kenneth, *Landscape into Art* (London: J. Murray, 1950).

Cornell, Kenneth, *The Post-Symbolist Period* (New Haven, Conn.: Yale University Press, 1958).

———, *The Symbolist Movement* (New Haven, Conn.: Yale University Press, 1951).

Day-Lewis, Cecil, *The Poetic Image* (London: Jonathan Cape, 1947).

Décaudin, Michel, *La Crise des valeurs symbolistes, vingt ans de poésie française, 1895–1914* (Toulouse: Privat, 1960).

Dodd, Charles Harold, *The Parables of the Kingdom*, Rev. ed. (New York: Scribner, 1961).

Janet, Pierre, *L'Evolution de la mémoire et de la notion du temps* (Paris: A. Cahine, 1928).

Lehmann, A. G., *The Symbolist Aesthetic in France, 1885–1895* (Oxford: Basil Blackwood, 1950).

Leibnitz, Gottfried W., *New Essays concerning Human Understanding*, trans. Alfred Gideon Langley (New York: Macmillan, 1896).

Michaud, Guy, *Message poétique du Symbolisme*, 4 vols. (Paris: Nizet, 1947).

Pépin, Jean, *Mythe et allégorie, les origines grecques et les contestations judéo-chrétiennes* (Paris: Editions Montaigne, 1958).

Schopenhauer, Arthur, *The World as Will and Idea*, trans. R. B. Haldane and J. Kemp, 3 vols. (London: Kegan Paul, 1907).

Smith, B. T. D., *The Parables of the Synoptic Gospels* (Cambridge, Eng.: Cambridge University Press, 1937).

Taine, Hippolyte, *De l'Idéal en art* (Paris: Baillère, 1867).

Tindall, William York, *The Literary Symbol* (Magnolia, Mass.: Peter Smith, 1955).

Wheelwright, Philip, *Metaphor and Reality* (Bloomington: Indiana University Press, 1962).

———, *The Burning Fountain, a Study in the Language of Symbolism* (Bloomington: Indiana University Press, 1954).

Index

"Agenda," 51

"Allain," 22, 27, 40

Amiel, Henri-Frédéric (*Fragments d'un journal intime*), 70, 166

Anachronism, as a literary device, 131, 132, 154

"Angèle, ou le pauvre petit voyage," 117, 128, 153

Arabian Nights, The, 77–78, 137, 168

Aristotle, 139

Arnheim, Rudolf ("The Robin and the Saint: on the Twofold Nature of the Artistic Image"), 137–38

Auerbach, Erich (*Mimesis*), 141–42

Barrès, Maurice, 51, 81, 169

Bashkirtseff, Marie (*Journal*), 31, 166

Baudelaire, Charles, 34, 36, 173

Bible, the, 14, 44–46, 50, 79, 80, 111, 135, 137 141–42

Bowra, C. M., 140

Brée, Germaine, 61, 80, 81, 88, 138–39, 180, 184

"Cahier de notes de lectures," 18, 31, 164

Cahiers d'André Walter, Les, 11, 12, 18, 22, 23, 24–37, 38–39, 40, 42–51, 53, 57, 58, 60, 61, 65, 68, 69, 72–74, 76, 83, 85, 99, 102, 114, 125, 129, 136, 152, 159, 160, 167, 184; faults of, 26, 30; Gide's justification of, 49–50; preface to the 1930 edition, 38–39; preparation of manuscript, 165; reception of, 30–31, 166

Calderón de la Barca, 174

Caractères, 39

Composition in a work of art, 26, 114, 115, 116, 118, 120, 138, 154

"Considérations sur la mythologie grecque," 133, 135

Curel, François de, 119–20

Day-Lewis, Cecil (*The Poetic Image*), 12, 14

"De l'influence en littérature," 126, 175

Delay, Jean (*La Jeunesse d'André Gide*), 4, 6–7, 27, 52, 53, 58, 79, 103, 151–52, 160

Descartes, René, 105, 107

Dostoïevsky, 159, 175

Drouin, Marcel, letter to Gide, 62; letters from Gide, 133, 183

Emotion in art, 66–68, 70–74 *passim*, 81, 84, 91–93, 97, 136
"En abyme" as a literary device, 129, 132, 147
Ermitage, L' (review), 99, 111, 119
"Evolution du théâtre, L'" 131–32, 134

Faux-Monnayeurs, Les, 13, 29, 154, 157–59
Fichte, Johann, 183
Flaubert, Gustave, 11, 20, 27, 81, 157
Freud, Sigmund, 7, 164

Gide, André, at Annecy (Menthon), 23, 24, 165; at Yport, 100, 176; didacticism, 183; difficulty with reality, 3, 4, 7–14 *passim*, 18, 21, 26; expression of emotion, 13, 14, 18, 24, 30, 53, 65, 71, 73, 80, 85, 87, 88, 98, 102; first trip to North Africa, 3, 11, 82, 99–102 *passim*, 122, 160, 174, 176; influence of Protestant background, 10, 115, 141; lack of sense of time, 5–8; realism, 184; Symbolist period, 51–52, 97, 99, 100, 107, 122, 176
Gide, Madeleine, 23–24, 30, 57, 102, 180
Goethe, Johann Wolfgang von, 103, 125; *Leiden des jungen Werthers*, 26, 39
Greeks, the, 133–36, 141, 142

Hennebert, Jean-Michel ("Du Prométhée à l'art d'André Gide"), 138–39, 141
Hytier, Jean, *André Gide*, 26, 35; *Le Plaisir poétique, Les Arts de la littérature*, 165–66

Idea, 19, 41, 42, 50, 55–56, 58, 60, 66, 113, 116, 122, 125, 126, 132, 138, 141, 144–54 *passim*, 159, 178, 184; in a work of art, 117–20, 132, 138; in Leibniz's definition of knowledge, 177; innate, 105–07, 177; Platonic versus Leibnizian, 107–08, 113, 152
"Ideorealism" (Mauclair), 152, 183
Image, 12, 14, 15, 20, 21, 65, 68, 69, 72, 73–74, 80–81, 84, 85–88, 90, 92, 95, 98, 134, 136, 140, 143, 144–46, 150, 159; according to Arnheim, 182; according to Schopenhauer, 20, 168
"Imagination," 117–18, 120, 144, 146, 153
Immoraliste, L', 117–19, 123, 150, 153, 154–57, 160, 180–81
Intuition, 17–21 *passim*, 24
Isabelle, 154, 157–58

Jammes, Francis, 100
Janet, Pierre, 5, 6, 7, 163
Journal, quotations from unpublished pages, 21, 117, 151–52, 163, 164–65, 176
Journal des Faux-Monnayeurs, 125

Knowledge, Leibniz's definition of, 177

Index

La Bruyère, Jean de, 110, 111, 116
Landscape, 69, 70–72, 74, 81, 84, 87–88, 92, 93, 97, 136, 150
Lang, Renée, 103–04
Laurens, Paul-Albert, 100, 174
Leibniz, Gottfreid W., 72, 103, 108, 123, 177, 178; *Nouveaux essais sur l'entendement humain*, 104–07, 108, 113, 122; *Théodicée*, 103
Lessing, Gotthold E., 177
"Lettre à Angèle," 119, 121
"Likeness" (Arnheim), 137–38, 144, 145, 182
"Limites de l'art, Les," 13, 175
Litotes, 53, 136
Littérature et morale, 108–10, 112–23, 124, 125, 127, 138
Locke, John, 105–07
Louÿs, Pierre, 21, 22, 24, 36, 102, 133

Maeterlinck, Maurice, 31, 51, 81
Maine de Biran, 72
Mallarmé, Stéphane, 20, 30–31, 51, 53, 61, 164; "Azur," 76
Martin-Chauffier, Louis, 82, 135
Mauclair, Camille, 129–30, 151, 183–84
Memling, Hans, 129

Notes d'un voyage en Bretagne, 27, 70–71, 166, 172
Nourritures terrestres, Les, 87, 99, 101, 123, 133
"Nouvelle Education sentimentale, La," 22, 26–27, 29
Novalis, 78, 173

O'Brien, Justin, 77–78, 83
Oedipe, 133, 146

Paludes, 14, 15, 87–98, 99, 101, 103, 104, 117, 118–20, 127–33, 136–47 *passim*, 150, 153–54, 159, 160, 183; Preface, 103
Parable, 139, 140, 141–42, 143; biblical, 142, 145, 147; Gidian, 145, 147, 149, 153, 154, 156, 159, 160, 183
"Pathetic fallacy," 63–81 *passim*
Perséphone, 133
Peyre, Henri, 103
Philoctète, 130, 132, 133, 146, 149–50
Pierre-Quint, Léon, 135
Plato, 139, 182
Poésies d'André Walter, Les, 38, 53, 74–77, 80, 84, 85, 97, 172, 174–75
Porte étroite, La, 118, 126, 146, 153–56, 179
Pretext, 32, 35, 95, 135, 165, 166
Prométhée mal enchaîné, Le, 130, 132, 146–50, 154
Proserpine, 133

Racine, Jean, 131
Réflexions sur quelques points de littérature et morale, see *Littérature et morale*
Renan, Ernest, 71–72
Retour de l'enfant prodigue, Le, 135, 146
Rimbaud, Arthur, 64, 78
Roi Candaule, Le, 130, 132, 146, 154; preface, 130
Ruskin, John, 70

Sainte-Beuve, Charles Augustin, 28
Saül, 123, 130, 146, 150, 154

Scenario, 116, 117, 118, 153, 154

Scheffer, letter from Gide, 84, 96

Schopenhauer, Arthur, 18, 19, 20, 24, 41–42, 48, 50, 164, 168

"Self-image" (Arnheim), 137–38, 145, 182

Simile, 20, 142–43

Smith, B. T. D., 142

Stevenson, Robert Louis, 137, 168

Symbol, 20, 21, 40–61 *passim*, 69–74, 86–88, 90–91, 95, 96, 118, 119, 130, 144, 153, 168, 170

Symbolism, 11, 97, 100

Symbolists, 51, 52, 61, 63; doctrine, 10, 87

Symphonie pastorale, La, 156, 157, 158

Tentative amoureuse, La: Traité du vain désir, 14, 82–87, 88, 97, 100–01, 129, 174, 176; preface, 82, 83

Théorie du symbole, 40, 60; see *Traité du Narcisse, Le*

Thésée, 133, 146

Thibaudet, Albert, 138–39

Thierry, Jean-Jacques, 82

Traité du Narcisse, Le, 40, 52, 53–62, 63, 65, 66, 67, 72, 73, 82, 85, 88, 108–116 *passim*, 129, 144, 152, 172, 180, 184

Ullman, Stephen, 81

Valéry, Paul, 4, 6, 51, 53–54, 60, 80–81, 104, 115, 180

Vergil (First *Eclogue*), 89, 131, 133

Verlaine, Paul, 47, 49

Voyage d'Urien, Le, 63–81, 82–88 *passim* 97, 173; chapter divisions, 171; preface, 67–71

Wilde, Oscar, 53, 71, 172

Zola, Emile, 11, 164, 184